Past Masters
General Editor Keith Thomas

Hegel

Peter Singer

HEGEL

Oxford   New York

OXFORD UNIVERSITY PRESS

1983

Oxford University Press, Walton Street, Oxford OX2 6DP

London Glasgow New York Toronto
Delhi Bombay Calcutta Madras Karachi
Kuala Lumpur Singapore Hong Kong Tokyo
Nairobi Dar es Salaam Cape Town
Melbourne Auckland
and associates in
Beirut Berlin Ibadan Mexico City Nicosia

British Library Cataloguing in Publication Data
Singer, Peter
Hegel.
1. Hegel, Georg Wilhelm Friedrich
I. Title II. Series
193   B2948
ISBN 0-19-287565-5
ISBN 0-19-287564-7 Pbk

Library of Congress Cataloging in Publication Data
Singer, Peter.
Hegel.
(Past masters)
Bibliography: p.
Includes index.
1. Hegel, George Wilhelm Friedrich, 1770–1831.
I. Title. II. Series.
B2948.S56 1983 193 82-14240
ISBN 0-19-287565-5
ISBN 0-19-287564-7 (pbk.)

Set by Datamove Ltd
Printed in Great Britain
at the University Press, Oxford
by Eric Buckley
Printer to the University

In memory of my father, Ernest Singer

Preface

No philosopher of the nineteenth or twentieth centuries has had as great an impact on the world as Hegel. The only possible exception to this sweeping statement would be Karl Marx – and Marx himself was heavily influenced by Hegel. Without Hegel, neither the intellectual nor the political developments of the last 150 years would have taken the path they did.

Hegel's impact alone makes it important to understand him; but Hegel's philosophy is in any case worth studying for its own sake. His profound ideas led him to some conclusions that strike the modern reader as bizarre, even absurd. Whatever one thinks of his conclusions, however, there are arguments and insights in his work that retain their force to the present day. The effort required to understand Hegel is repaid by them, and also by the satisfaction of having mastered the challenge to our comprehension that Hegel represents.

That Hegel does present a challenge is undeniable. Commentaries on Hegel are studded with references to the 'Himalayan severity' of his prose, to his 'repulsive terminology' and to the 'extreme obscurity' of his thought. To illustrate the nature of the problem I have just now picked up my copy of what many consider to be his greatest work, *The Phenomenology of Mind*, and opened it at random. The first complete sentence on the page on which it opened (p. 596) reads: 'It is merely the restless shifting change of those moments, of which one is indeed being-returned-into-itself, but merely as being-for-itself, i.e. as abstract moment, appearing on one side over against the others.' Admittedly, I have wrenched the sentence from its context; even so, it indicates some of the difficulties one has in making sense of Hegel. Equally formidable sentences can be found on every one of the *Phenomenology*'s 750 pages.

To explain the work of such a philosopher in a short book intended for an audience with no prior knowledge of his work is no easy task. To make the task a little more manageable, I have done two things. The first is to limit the scope. I have not attempted to give an account of all of Hegel's thought. So the reader will find here no account of what Hegel said in his *Lectures on Aesthetics*, nor of his *Lectures on the History of Philosophy*, nor of his *Lectures on the Philosophy of Religion*, nor of anything in his *Encyclopedia of the Philosophical Sciences*, except where these works overlap with other works that are discussed. (In the case of the *Encyclopedia* the overlap is considerable, the major section not covered elsewhere being that on the philosophy of nature.) These omissions are significant, of course, but I console myself with the thought that Hegel himself would not have considered them absolutely central to his philosophical system. More serious, however, is the absence of any detailed account of Hegel's *Science of Logic*, which he undoubtedly did consider a key work. I have tried to give something of the aim, method and flavour of it, but the *Logic* is so very long and so very abstract that an adequate account is, in my view, beyond the scope of any 100-page introduction to Hegel.

The second part of my strategy for making the lofty heights of Hegel's thought accessible to novices is to select the gentlest possible approach route. Accordingly I begin with the most concrete, least abstract, part of Hegel's thought, his philosophy of history. From there, still remaining on the social and political level, we move upwards to his views of freedom and the rational organisation of society. Only then do we attempt the rocky pinnacles of the *Phenomenology*, after which our ascent a short way up the *Logic* will take little extra effort.

Hegel scholars may object to the selection of works I have chosen to discuss, or to the order in which I discuss them. I have already indicated that the order is not intended to suggest anything about how Hegel himself would have chosen to present his ideas. As for the selection, I do not pretend that Hegel thought his *Lectures on the Philosophy of History* any more important than, say, the section of his *Encyclopedia* on the philosophy of nature. All I know is that I do not have space to discuss them both, and I am certain that Hegel's philosophy of history has been more important to the development of modern thought, and remains to this day far more interesting to the general reader, than his philosophy of nature. (Don't be misled by the title: Hegel's philosophy of nature does not contain his musings upon the value and beauty of forests and mountains. It is Hegel's attempt to show how the findings of the natural sciences − physics, chemistry, biology etc. − conform to his logical categories. Much of what Hegel said has since been rendered obsolete: for example his view that nature cannot develop is falsified by our knowledge of evolution.) My selection has therefore been influenced by three separate factors: what is central to Hegel's thought, what can be rendered intelligible to the general reader within the length of this volume, and what remains interesting and important to people living in the late twentieth century.

For the view of Hegel expressed in the following pages I am indebted to many people. At Oxford I was fortunate to be able to attend two remarkable series of classes offered by J. L. H. Thomas, who forced his students to probe passages of the *Phenomenology* sentence by sentence, until they yielded their meaning. The detailed work we did in those classes was admirably complemented by the broader brushwork of Patrick Gardiner's lectures on German Idealism. My other debts are to the authors of books from which I have freely plundered their best (I hope) ideas. Most prominent among these are Richard Norman's *Hegel's Phenomenology*, Ivan Soll's *An Introduction to Hegel's Metaphysics*, and two books entitled *Hegel*, one by Walter Kaufmann and the other by Charles Taylor. Bob Solomon read the typescript and suggested some improvements, as did Henry Hardy, Keith Thomas and an anonymous O.U.P. reader.

It remains only to thank Jean Archer for her excellent typing, and Ruth, Marion and Esther for allowing me some time to work during their summer holidays.

PETER SINGER

Melbourne, Australia
March 1982

Contents

1 Hegel's times and life

Hegel's times

George Wilhelm Friedrich Hegel was born in Stuttgart in 1770. His father was a minor civil servant at the court of the Duchy of Württemberg. Other relatives were teachers or Lutheran ministers. There is nothing particularly extraordinary to relate about his life, but the times in which he lived were momentous, politically, culturally and philosophically.

In 1789 news of the fall of the Bastille reverberated around Europe. It is of this moment that Wordsworth wrote:

> Bliss was it in that dawn to be alive,
> But to be young was very heaven!

Hegel was just short of his nineteenth birthday. He too was later to call the French Revolution a 'glorious dawn' and to add: 'All thinking beings shared in the jubilation of this epoch.' Sharing in it himself one Sunday morning in spring, he went out with some fellow students to plant a liberty tree, a symbol of the hopes sown by the Revolution.

By the time Hegel was twenty-one, the Revolutionary Wars had begun, and Germany was soon to be invaded by the revolutionary armies. The area we now know as Germany then consisted of more than 300 States, duchies and free cities, loosely linked together as the Holy Roman Empire under the leadership of Francis I of Austria. Napoleon put an end to this thousand-year-old empire when he trounced the Austrians at Ulm and Austerlitz, and then in 1806 crushed the armies of the next most powerful German State, Prussia, at the battle of Jena. Hegel was living in Jena at the time. One might have expected his sympathies to have been with the defeated German State, but a letter he wrote the day after Jena was occupied by the French shows only admiration for Napoleon: 'The Emperor − this world soul − I saw riding through the city to review his troops; it is indeed a wonderful feeling to see such an individual who, here concentrated into a single point, sitting on a horse, reaches out over the world and dominates it.'

This admiration remained throughout the period in which Napoleon ruled over Europe; and when in 1814 Napoleon was defeated, Hegel referred to this as a tragic thing, the spectacle of an immense genius destroyed by mediocrity.

The period of French power, between 1806 and 1814, was a period of reform in Germany. In Prussia, von Stein, a liberal, was appointed chief adviser to the king, and immediately abolished serfdom and reorganised the system of government. He was followed by von Hardenberg, who promised to give Prussia a representative constitution; but after Napoleon's defeat these hopes were dashed. The Prussian king, Frederick William III, lost interest in reform and in 1823, after years of delay, set up only provisional 'estates' which could do no more than advise, and in any case were completely dominated by landowners. Moreover in 1819, at a meeting at Carlsbad, all the German States agreed to censor newspapers and periodicals and to adopt repressive measures against those who advocated revolutionary ideas.

From a cultural point of view, Hegel lived in the golden age of German literature. Twenty years younger than Goethe and ten years younger than Schiller, he was nevertheless old enough to appreciate all of their mature works as they appeared. He was a close friend of the poet Hölderlin, and a contemporary of the leaders of the German Romantic movement, including Novalis, Herder, Schleiermacher and the Schlegel brothers. Goethe and Schiller were major influences on Hegel, and he was obviously taken with some of the Romantic movement's ideas, though he rejected most of what the Romantics stood for.

Most significant of all for Hegel's development was the state of German philosophy in the period in which he worked. To appreciate the background to Hegel's own thought, we need to begin this story with Kant, and briefly sketch what happened thereafter.

Immanuel Kant published the *Critique of Pure Reason* in 1781. This is now regarded as one of the greatest philosophical works of all time. Kant set out to establish what our reason or intellect can or cannot achieve in the way of knowledge. He concluded that our mind is no merely passive receiver of information obtained by our eyes, ears and other senses. Knowledge is only possible because our mind plays an active role, organising and systematising what we experience. We know the world within a framework of space, time and substance; but space, time and substance are not objective realities that exist 'out there', independently of us. They are creations of our intuition or reason without which we could not comprehend the world. What, then, one might naturally ask, is the world really like, independently of the framework within which we grasp it? This question, Kant says, can never be answered. Independent reality — Kant called it the world of the 'thing-in-itself' — is for ever beyond our knowledge.

During Kant's lifetime it was not simply the *Critique of Pure Reason* that built his towering reputation. There were also two other critiques, the *Critique of Practical Reason*, on ethics, and the *Critique of Judgement*, a large part of which is on aesthetics. In the former, Kant pictured man as a being capable of following a rational moral law, but also liable to be swayed from it by the non-rational desires which have their origin in our physical nature. To act morally is thus always a struggle. Victory is to be won by the suppression of all desires except the feeling of reverence for the moral law, which leads us to do our duty for its own sake. In contrast to this view of morality as based only on the reasoning aspects of human nature, in the *Critique of Judgement* Kant pictured aesthetic appreciation as involving a harmonious union of our understanding and our imagination.

In the closing words of the *Critique of Pure Reason*, Kant expressed the hope that by following the path of critical philosophy that he had trodden, it might be possible 'before the present century runs out' to attain what many centuries before had been unable to achieve, namely 'to give human reason complete satisfaction about that which has always engaged its curiosity, but so far in vain'. So impressive was Kant's achievement that for a time it did indeed seem, not just to Kant but also to his readers, as if there were only a few more details to be filled in, and then all philosophy would be complete. Gradually, however, dissatisfaction with Kant began to be expressed.

The first source of dissatisfaction was Kant's view of the

'thing-in-itself'. That something should exist and yet be completely unknowable seemed an unsatisfactory limitation on the powers of human reason. And was not Kant contradicting himself when he said that we could know nothing of it, and yet claimed to know that it exists and is a 'thing'? It was Johann Fichte who took the bold step of denying the existence of the thing-in-itself, thus being more true to Kant's philosophy, he asserted, than Kant was himself. The whole world, in Fichte's view, was to be seen as something constituted by our active minds. What mind cannot know, does not exist.

The second source of dissatisfaction was the division of human nature implied by Kant's moral philosophy. Here it was Schiller who began the attack, in his *Lectures on the Aesthetic Education of Man*. He too saw himself as using Kant to improve upon Kant, for he borrowed from the *Critique of Judgement* the model of aesthetic judgement as a unity of understanding and imagination. Surely, said Schiller, all our life should be similarly harmonious. To portray human nature as for ever divided between reason and passion, and our moral life as an eternal struggle between the two, is degrading and defeatist. Perhaps, Schiller suggested, Kant was accurately describing the sorry state of human life today, but it was not always so and it need not always be so. In ancient Greece, so much admired for the purity of its artistic forms, there had been a harmonious unity between reason and passion. To serve as a basis of a restoration of that long-lost harmony in human nature, Schiller therefore urged the revival of the sense of the aesthetic in every aspect of life.

Hegel was later to write that Kant's philosophy 'constitutes the basis and point of departure for modern German philosophy'. We could add that Fichte and Schiller, in their different ways, showed the directions these departures were to take. The unknowable thing-in-itself and the conception of human nature divided against itself were both, for Kant's successors, problems in need of solutions.

In an early essay, Hegel expressed his admiration for Schiller's objections to Kant's view of human nature, and especially for the point that this disharmony was not an eternal truth about human nature, but a problem to be overcome. He could not accept, however, the idea that aesthetic education was the way to overcome it. Instead he regarded the task as one for philosophy.

Hegel's life

After doing unusually well at school, Hegel won a scholarship to a well-known seminary at Tübingen, where he studied philosophy and theology. Here he became friendly with the poet Hölderlin and with a younger, very talented student of philosophy named Friedrich Schelling. Schelling was to achieve a national reputation as a philosopher before anyone had heard of Hegel; later, when his reputation had been eclipsed by that of Hegel, he was to complain that his former friend had taken over his own ideas. Though Schelling is little read nowadays, the parallels between his views and Hegel's are sufficiently close to lend the complaint some plausibility, provided we overlook how much more Hegel made of the points on which the two concurred.

After completing his studies at Tübingen, Hegel accepted a post as family tutor with a wealthy family in Switzerland. This was followed by a similar position in Frankfurt. During this period Hegel continued to read and think about philosophical questions. He wrote essays on religion, not for publication but to clarify his thoughts. The essays show him to have been thinking along radical lines. Jesus is compared with Socrates, and emerges from the comparison as decidedly the inferior teacher of ethics. Orthodox religion is, in Hegel's eyes, a barrier to the goal of restoring man to a state of harmony, for it makes man subordinate his own powers of thought to an external authority. For the rest of his life, Hegel retained something of this attitude to orthodox religion; yet his radicalism ebbed to the extent that, later on, he could consider himself a Lutheran Christian and regularly attend Lutheran church services.

When his father died in 1799 Hegel found himself with a modest inheritance. He gave up tutoring and joined his friend Schelling at the University of Jena, in the small state of Weimar. Schiller and Fichte had been at Jena, and Schelling was now also well-known; Hegel, on the other hand, had published virtually nothing and had to be content to lecture privately, supplementing his capital only by the small fees he collected from the few students (eleven in 1801, thirty by 1804) who came to hear him.

At Jena, Hegel published a long pamphlet on the differences between the philosophies of Fichte and Schelling: in every case, in his opinion, Schelling's view was to be preferred. For a time he worked with Schelling on a *Critical Journal of Philosophy*, for which he wrote several essays. In 1803 Schelling left Jena, and Hegel began to prepare his first major work, *The Phenomenology of Mind*. His inheritance now exhausted, he was badly in need of money. He accepted a publisher's contract which provided him with a cash advance but contained draconian penalty clauses if he should fail to post the manuscript by the due date of 13 October 1806. This turned out to be the day Jena was occupied by the French following their victory over the Prussians. Hegel had to rush the final sections of the book in order to meet his deadline, and then to his consternation found that he had no alternative but to send off the manuscript – his only copy – amidst all the confusion caused by the arrival of the warring armies outside Jena. Luckily the manuscript travelled undisturbed and the work appeared early in 1807.

The initial reaction was respectful, if hardly enthusiastic. Schelling was understandably perturbed to find that the preface contained a polemical attack on what seemed to be his views. In a letter Hegel explained that he intended to criticise not Schelling but only his unworthy imitators. Schelling replied that this distinction was not made in the preface itself, and refused to be mollified. Their friendship was at an end.

Life at Jena had been disrupted by the French occupation. Now that the university had closed down, Hegel worked for a year as a newspaper editor, and then accepted the headmastership of the academic high school at Nuremberg. He remained in this post for nine years, and made a success of it. In addition to the more usual subjects, he taught his schoolboys philosophy. What they made of his lectures is not known.

In Nuremberg Hegel's domestic life became settled. At Jena he had fathered an illegitimate son, the mother being his landlady, who is recorded as having had two previous illegitimate children by other lovers. In 1811, aged forty-one, Hegel married the daughter of an old Nuremberg family. She was scarcely half his age, but the marriage was, as far as one can tell, a happy one. They had two sons, and after the death of the mother of Hegel's first child, his wife was sufficiently tolerant to take his illegitimate son into her household as well.

During these years Hegel published his lengthy *Science of Logic*, which appeared in three volumes in 1812, 1813 and 1816. His works were now gaining wider appreciation, and in 1816 he was invited to take the post of Professor of Philosophy at the University of Heidelberg. Here he wrote the *Encyclopedia of the Philosophical Sciences*, which is a relatively brief statement of his entire philosophical system. Much of the material in it is also contained, in amplified form, in his other works.

Hegel's reputation was now so high that the Prussian Minister of Education asked him to take up the prestigious chair of philosophy at the University of Berlin. The Prussian educational system had benefited from the reforms of von Stein and von Hardenberg, and Berlin was becoming the intellectual centre of all the German States. Hegel accepted the offer with alacrity, and taught at Berlin from 1818 until he died in 1831.

In every respect this final period was the climax of Hegel's life. He wrote and published his *Philosophy of Right* and lectured on the philosophy of history, the philosophy of religion, aesthetics and the history of philosophy. He was not a good lecturer in the conventional sense, but he clearly captivated his students. Here is a description by one of them:

> I was unable at first to find my way into either the manner of his delivery or the train of his thought. Exhausted, morose, he sat there as if collapsed into himself, his head bent down, and while speaking kept turning pages and searching in his folio notebooks, forward and backward, high and low. His constant clearing of his throat and coughing interrupted any flow of speech. Every sentence stood alone and came out with effort, cut in pieces and jumbled ... Eloquence that flows along smoothly presupposes that the speaker is finished with the subject inside and out and has it by heart ... this man, however, had to raise up the most powerful thoughts from the deepest ground of things ... a more vivid representation of these difficulties and this immense trouble than was

accomplished by the manner of his delivery would be inconceivable.

Hegel was now attracting large audiences. People came to hear him from all over the German-speaking world, and many of the brightest became his disciples. After his death they were to edit and publish his lecture notebooks, supplemented by additions from their own notes of what he had said. It is in this way that several of Hegel's works – the *Lectures on the Philosophy of History*, the *Lectures on Aesthetics*, the *Lectures on the Philosophy of Religion* and the *Lectures on the History of Philosophy* – have come down to us.

In 1830, in recognition of his status, Hegel was elected Rector of the University. The following year, at the age of sixty-one, he suddenly fell ill and the next day died in his sleep. 'What an awful void!' wrote one of his colleagues: 'He was the cornerstone of our university.'

2 History with a purpose

Hegel took history seriously. In contrast to Kant, who thought he could say on purely philosophical grounds what human nature is and always must be, Hegel accepted Schiller's suggestion that the very foundations of the human condition could change from one historical era to another. This notion of change, of development throughout history, is fundamental to Hegel's view of the world. Friedrich Engels, looking back on Hegel's importance to himself and to his colleague Karl Marx, wrote:

> What distinguished Hegel's mode of thinking from that of all other philosophers was the exceptional historical sense underlying it. However abstract and idealist the form employed, the development of his ideas runs always parallel to the development of world history, and the latter is indeed supposed to be only the proof of the former.

We need not yet concern ourselves about the meaning of Engels's last clause − the reference to the development of world history as the 'proof' of Hegel's system of ideas − for the undoubted parallel between the development of Hegel's ideas and the development of world history to which Engels draws attention is sufficient justification for using Hegel's understanding of world history as our way into his system of ideas.

The other point to be drawn from what Engels says is simply that in assessing the importance of Hegel's influence on Marx and himself, he gives first place to Hegel's historical sense. So in beginning our introduction with Hegel's *Philosophy of History*, we are beginning with a topic that is central not only to Hegel's system, but also to the enduring influence of his ideas.

What is philosophy of history?

It is first necessary to understand what a 'philosophy of history' is, in Hegel's sense of the term. Hegel's *Philosophy of History* contains a good deal of historical information. One can find in it a kind of outline of world history, from the early civilisations of China, India and Persia, through ancient Greece to Roman times, and then tracing the path of European history from feudalism to the Reformation and on to the Enlightenment and the French Revolution. Yet Hegel obviously did not think of his *Philosophy of History* as merely a historical outline. His work is a work of philosophy because it takes the bare facts of history as its raw material, and attempts to go beyond these facts. Hegel himself said that 'the philosophy of history means nothing but the thoughtful consideration of it'. While this may be his own definition, however, it conveys a less than adequate idea of what Hegel is up to in his *Philosophy of History*. What Hegel's definition leaves out is his intention that the 'thoughtful consideration' of history should seek to present its raw material as part of a rational process of development, thus revealing the meaning and significance of world history.

Here, already, we have one of Hegel's central beliefs – the belief that history has some meaning and significance. Had Hegel viewed history along the lines of Macbeth's bleak vision of life, that is, as 'a tale told by an idiot, full of sound and fury, signifying nothing', he would never have attempted to write the *Philosophy of History* and his life's work would have been unrecognisably different. The modern scientific view is, of course, much like Macbeth's. It tells us that our planet is just one tiny speck in a universe of unimaginable size; and that on this planet life began from a chance combination of gases and then evolved by the blind forces of natural selection. Consistently with this view of the origin of our species, most modern thought refuses to assume that history has any ultimate purpose beyond the myriad individual purposes of the countless human beings who make history. In Hegel's day there was nothing unusual about his confident belief that human history is not a meaningless jumble of events – indeed, it is not really out of the ordinary even now, for religious thought has traditionally seen meaning and significance in the course taken by human history, even if it has significance only as a prelude to a better world still to come.

There are many different ways in which the claim that history is meaningful may be understood. It may be taken as a claim that history is the working out of the purposes of some Creator who set the whole process in motion; or, more mysteriously, it may be intended to suggest that the universe itself can somehow have purposes. The assertion that history has a meaning can also be shorn of all religious or mystical connotations and understood simply as the more limited claim that reflection on our past enables us to discern the direction history is taking, and the destination it will ultimately reach; this destination, for some fortunate reason, being a desirable one and hence one we can accept as the goal of our own strivings.

It is possible to interpret Hegel's *Philosophy of History* in different ways, corresponding to these different ways of understanding the claim that there is a meaning to history. In accordance with our general strategy of coming to grips with Hegel, we shall begin with those elements of the work that endow history with a meaning in the third, and least mysterious, of the various ways of understanding the claim.

In his own introduction to the *Philosophy of History*, Hegel clearly states his view of the direction and destination of all human history: 'The history of the world is none other than the progress of the consciousness of freedom.' This sentence sets the theme for the entire work. (One might even say that it sums up the theme of *all* of Hegel's thought – but more of that later.) Now we must see how Hegel elaborates upon his theme.

He begins with an account of what he calls 'The Oriental World' – by which he means China, India and the ancient empire of Persia. China and India Hegel regards as 'stationary' civilisations, societies that have reached a certain point of their development and then somehow stuck fast. He describes them as 'outside the World's History', in other words not part of the overall process of development that is the basis of his philosophy of history. True history begins with the Persian Empire, 'the first Empire', says Hegel, 'that passed away'.

Hegel's discussion of the Oriental world contains many points of detail, all related to the idea that in oriental society only one person – the ruler – is a free individual. All others are totally lacking in freedom, because they must subordinate their will to that of the Patriarch, Lama, Emperor, Pharaoh, or whatever else the despot may be called. This lack of freedom goes very deep. It is not simply that the subjects of the despot know that the despot can punish them cruelly for disobeying his will. This would imply that they have wills of their own, that they can and do think about whether it is prudent or right to obey the despot. The truth is, says Hegel, that the oriental subject has no will of his own in the modern sense. In the Orient not only law, but even morality itself, is a matter of external regulation. Our concept of individual conscience is lacking. Hence there is no sense of the possibility of individuals forming their own moral judgements about right and wrong. For the inhabitants of the Orient − other than the ruler − opinions on these matters come from outside; they are facts about the world, and no more to be questioned than the existence of the mountains and the seas.

This lack of personal independence takes different forms in different oriental cultures, according to Hegel, but the result is always the same. The Chinese State, Hegel tells us, is organised on the principle of the family. Government is based on the paternal management of the Emperor, and all others see themselves as children of the State. It is for this reason that Chinese society places such strong emphasis on the honour and obedience one owes to one's parents. India, in contrast, has no concept of individual freedom because the basic institution of society − the caste system which allocates to each his or her occupation in life − is not seen as a political institution, but as something natural and hence unchangeable. The governing power in India is therefore not a human despot, but the despotism of nature.

Persia is different. Although at first glance the Persian Emperor seems to be an absolute ruler in much the same sense as the Emperor of China, the basis of the Persian Empire is not merely natural family obedience extended to the entire State, but a general principle, a Law which regulates the rules as well as the subject. For Persia was a theocratic monarchy, based on the religion of Zoroaster, which involved the worship of Light. Hegel makes much of the idea of light as something pure and universal, something which, like the sun, shines on all and confers equal benefits on all. Of course this does not mean that Persia was egalitarian. The Emperor was still an absolute ruler and hence the only free man in the Empire; yet the fact that his rule was based on a general principle and was not seen as a natural fact meant that development was possible. The idea of rule based on an intellectual or spiritual principle signifies the beginning of the growth of the consciousness of freedom that Hegel intends to trace. Hence it is the beginning of 'true history'.

The Greek world

In the Persian Empire the potential for growth in the consciousness of freedom existed; but this potential could not be realised within the structure of the Empire. In its efforts to expand, however, the Persian Empire came into contact with Athens, 'Sparta and the other city-states of ancient Greece. The Persian Emperor asked the Greeks to acknowledge his supremacy. They refused. The Emperor assembled an enormous army and a vast fleet of ships. The Persian fleet and the Greek fleet met at Salamis. This epic battle, Hegel says, was a contest between an oriental despot who sought a world united under one lord and sovereign, and separate States that recognised the principle of 'free individuality'. The Greek victory meant that the tide of world history passed from the despotic oriental world to the world of the Greek city-states.

While Hegel sees the Greek world as animated by the idea of free individuality, it is his view that the freedom of the individual is by no means fully developed at this stage of history. He has two different reasons for regarding the Greek idea of freedom as a limited one. One of these reasons is straightforward and the other is more complex.

The straightforward reason is that the Greek idea of freedom allows slavery. Indeed, 'allows' is too weak a term, for in Hegel's view the Greek form of democracy positively required slavery if it was to function at all. If, as was the case in Athens, every citizen has the right and duty to take part in the public assembly that is the supreme decision-making body of the city-state, then who is there to do the daily work of providing the necessities of life? There must be a category of workers who lack the rights and duties of citizens – in other words, there must be slaves.

In the oriental world only *one* – the ruler – is free. The

existence of slavery means that the Greek world has progressed to a stage at which *some* – not all – are free. But even those who are free citizens of a Greek city-state are only free, Hegel believes, in an incomplete way. His reason for saying this is not so easy to grasp. He claims that the Greeks had no concept of individual conscience. This concept, as we have seen, Hegel thought to be lacking in the oriental world too; but whereas in the Orient people simply obeyed, without reflection, a moral code that was handed down to them from on high, with the Greeks the motivation came from inside themselves. They had, according to Hegel, the habit of living for their country, without further reflection. This habit did not derive from the acceptance of some abstract principle, such as the idea that everyone should act for the sake of his or her country. Rather the Greeks habitually thought of themselves as so indissolubly linked with their own particular city-state that they did not distinguish between their own interests and the interests of the community in which they lived. They could not conceive of themselves as living apart from, or in opposition to, this community, with all its customs and forms of social life.

All this means that the readiness of the Greeks to do what is best for the community as a whole comes from within. This would suggest that the Greeks were free in a way in which the Orientals were not. They did as they themselves wished to do, not as some external decree required them to do. Yet Hegel says that this is an incomplete form of freedom just because the motivation comes so naturally. Whatever is the result of the habits and customs in which one was brought up is not the result of the use of one's reason. If I do something from habit, I have not deliberately chosen to do it. My actions, it might be said, are still governed by forces external to my will – the social forces that gave me my habits – even though there is no despot telling me what to do, and the motivation for the action appears to come from within.

As a symptom of this dependence on external forces Hegel refers to the Greek tendency to consult an oracle for guidance before any important venture is undertaken. The advice of the oracle might be based on the state of the intestines of a sacrificed animal, or on some other natural event quite independent of my own thought. Genuinely free people would not allow their most important decisions to be determined by such events; they would make their own decisions, using their capacity to reason. Reason lifts free people above the chance events of the natural world, and enables them to reflect critically upon their situation and the forces that influence them. Hence freedom cannot be fully achieved without critical thought and reflection.

Critical thought and reflection, then, is the key to further progress in the development of freedom. The command attributed to the Greek god Apollo urged the Greeks along this path: 'Man, know thyself.' This summons to free enquiry, untrammelled by customary beliefs, was taken up by the Greek philosophers, and especially by Socrates. Socrates typically expresses his own views in the form of a dialogue with some worthy Athenian who thinks that he knows well what is good or just. This 'knowledge' turns out to be merely the ability to echo some common saying about goodness or justice, and Socrates has no difficulty in showing that this customary conception of morality cannot be the full story. For example, against the common idea that justice consists in giving to each what is owed to him, Socrates poses the case of a friend who has lent you a weapon, but has since become deranged. You may owe him the weapon, but is it really just to return it? Thus Socrates leads his audience to critical reflection upon the customary morality they have always accepted. This critical reflection makes reason, not social custom, the final judge of right and wrong.

Hegel sees the principle exemplified by Socrates as a revolutionary force against the Athenian State. Thus he judges the death sentence passed upon Socrates as unimpeachably correct: the Athenian people were condemning the deadliest foe of the customary morality on which their communal existence was based. Yet the principle of independent thought was too firmly rooted in Athens to be extirpated by the death of one individual; and so in time the accusers of Socrates were condemned and Socrates himself posthumously exonerated. This principle of independent thought was, none the less, the ultimate cause of the downfall of Athens and marks the beginning of the end of the world-historical role played by the Greek civilisation.

The Roman world

In contrast to the ùnreflective customary unity which formed the basis of the Greek city-states, Hegel pictures the Roman Empire as built up from a collection of diverse peoples, lacking all natural patriarchal or other customary bonds, and hence requiring the most severe discipline, backed by force, to hold it together. This makes the dominance of Rome in the next stage of world history appear something of a reversion to the despotic oriental model, as typified in the Persian Empire. But while the course of world history, as Hegel presents it, is certainly not a smooth and steady progression, it does not go backwards either. The gains made in a previous epoch are never lost entirely. So Hegel carefully distinguishes between the underlying principles of the Persian and the Roman Empires. The idea of individuality, of the private capacity for judgement, that was born in the Greek era has not disappeared. Indeed, the Roman State rests upon a political constitution and a legal system which has individual right as one of its most fundamental notions. Thus the Roman State recognises individual freedom in a way that the Persian Empire never could; the catch is, of course, that this recognition of individual freedom is a purely legal or formal matter – Hegel calls it 'abstract freedom of the individual'. The real freedom that allows individuals to develop a diversity of ideas and ways of living – 'concrete individuality' in Hegel's terminology – is ruthlessly crushed by the brute power of Rome.

The real difference between the Persian and the Roman Empires, then, is that whereas in the former the principle of oriental despotism held unbridled sway, in the latter there is a constant tension between the absolute power of the State and the ideal of individuality. This tension was lacking in the Persian Empire because the ideal of individuality was yet to be developed; it was lacking in the Greek world because, while the idea of individuality had come to the fore, political power was not so ruthlessly centralised in opposition to it.

The Roman world, as Hegel paints it, is not a happy place. The joyous, spontaneous free spirit of the Greek world has been broken. In the face of the demands of the State for outward conformity, freedom can only be found by retreating into oneself, by taking refuge in a philosophy such as Stoicism, Epicureanism or Scepticism. The details of these opposing philosophical schools need not concern us here; what is important is their common tendency to pooh-pooh everything that the real world has to offer − riches, political power, worldly glory − and to substitute an ideal of living which makes the adherent absolutely indifferent to anything the outside world can do.

The spread of these philosophical schools was, according to Hegel, a result of the helplessness that the individual, who sees himself as a free being, must feel in the face of a domineering power he is unable to influence. The retreat into philosophy is, however, a negative response to this situation; it is a counsel of despair in the face of a hostile world. There was a need for a more positive solution. This solution was provided by Christianity.

To understand why Hegel sees Christianity in this way, we must appreciate that for Hegel human beings are not just very clever animals. Humans live in the natural world, as animals do, but they are also spiritual beings. Until they recognise themselves as spiritual beings, humans are trapped in the natural world, the world of material forces. When the natural world is implacably resistant to their aspiration for freedom, as the Roman world was, there is no escape *within* the natural world, apart from the already mentioned retreat into a philosophy based on a purely negative attitude towards the natural world. Once humans recognise themselves as spiritual beings, however, the hostility of the natural world ceases to be all-important; it can be transcended in a positive manner because there is something positive beyond the natural world.

The Christian religion is special, according to Hegel, because Jesus Christ was both a human being and the Son of God. This teaches humans that, though limited in some respects, they are at the same time made in the image of God and have within themselves an infinite value and an eternal destiny. The result is the development of what Hegel calls 'religious self-consciousness': a recognition that it is the spiritual world, not the natural world, that is our true home. To achieve this awareness humans have to break the hold that natural desires, and indeed the whole of natural existence, has over them.

It is the role of the Christian religion to achieve this awareness that the spiritual nature of human beings is what is essential to them. This does not, however, happen all at once; for it is not mere inner piety that is required. The change that takes place in the pious heart of the Christian believer must transform the real external world into something that satisfies the requirements of humans as spiritual beings. As we shall see, it takes the whole of the Christian era up to Hegel's own time for humanity to become capable of achieving this.

What does happen rather sooner is that the limitations on freedom characteristic of the Greek era are abolished. First, Christianity opposes slavery, for each unit of mankind has the same essential infinite value. Secondly, the dependence on oracles ceases, for oracles represent the dominance of the chance happenings of the natural world over the free choice of spiritual beings. Thirdly, and for much the same reason, the customary morality of Greek society is replaced by a morality based on the spiritual idea of love.

Christianity comes to the fore under the Roman Empire and becomes the official religion of the Empire under Constantine. Though the western half of the Empire falls to the barbarian invasions, the Byzantine Empire remains Christian for more than a thousand years. Yet this is, in Hegel's view, a stagnant, decadent Christianity, for it was an attempt to put a Christian veneer over structures that were already rotten to the core. It takes a new people to carry the Christian principle to its ultimate destiny.

The Germanic world

It may seem strange that Hegel should refer to the entire period of history from the fall of the Roman Empire up to modern times as 'The Germanic World'. He uses the term '*Germanische*' – 'Germanic' rather than simply 'German' – and he includes not only Germany proper, but also Scandinavia, the Netherlands, and even Britain. Nor, as we shall see, are developments in Italy and France ignored, though here he lacks the excuse of linguistic and racial affinities for stretching the term 'Germanic' to include these countries. One might suspect a certain amount of ethnocentrism in Hegel's designation of this era as 'The Germanic World'; but his chief reason for doing so is that he takes the Reformation as the single key event of history since Roman times.

Hegel paints a gloomy picture of Europe during the thousand years that passed after the fall of Rome. During that time the Church, in his view, became a perversion of the true religious spirit, inserting itself between man and the spiritual world, and insisting on blind obedience from its followers. The Middle Ages is, in Hegel's words, 'a long, eventful and terrible night'; a night which is ended by the Renaissance, 'that blush of dawn which after long storms first betokens the return of a bright and glorious day'. It is the Reformation, however, and not the Renaissance which Hegel describes as 'the all-enlightening Sun' of the bright day that is our modern time.

The Reformation resulted from the corruption of the Church, a corruption that was in Hegel's view not an accidental development but a necessary consequence of the fact that the Church does not treat the Deity as a purely spiritual thing, but instead embodies it in the material world. Ceremonial observances, rituals and other outward forms are its basis; and compliance with them is what it takes as essential to the religious life. Thus the spiritual element in human beings is fettered to mere material objects. The ultimate expression of this deep-seated corruption is the practice of selling, for that most worldly of objects, money, something that concerns man's deepest and inmost nature — the spiritual peace brought by the remission of sins. Hegel is of course referring to the practice of selling 'indulgences' which started Luther's protest.

Hegel sees the Reformation as an achievement of the Germanic people, arising from 'the honest truth and simplicity of its heart'. 'Simplicity' and 'heart' are for Hegel the keynotes of the Reformation, which was begun by the simple German monk, Luther, and took root only in the Germanic nations. Its result was to do away with the pomp and circumstance of the Roman Catholic Church and to substitute the idea that each individual human being has, in his own heart, a direct spiritual relationship to Christ.

It would be quite contrary to Hegel's view of the Reformation, however, to present it as an event within some isolated sphere of life labelled 'religion'. For one thing, Hegel always stresses the interrelatedness of different aspects of our historical development. For another, as we have already seen, for humans to fulfil their spiritual nature it is not enough for them to perfect their religious life; they must also make the world in which they live something suitable for free spiritual beings. Thus Hegel sees the Reformation as much more than an attack on the old Church, and the replacement of Roman Catholicism by Protestantism. The Reformation proclaims that every human being can recognise the truth of his or her own spiritual nature, and can achieve his or her own salvation. No outside authority is needed to interpret the scriptures, or to perform rituals. The individual conscience is the ultimate judge of truth and goodness. In asserting this, the Reformation unfurls 'the banner of Free Spirit' and proclaims as its essential principle: 'Man is in his very nature destined to be free.'

Since the Reformation, the role of history has been nothing but the transforming of the world in accordance with this essential principle. This is no small task, for if every human being is freely able to use his powers of reasoning to judge truth and goodness, the world can only receive universal assent when it conforms with rational standards. Therefore all social institutions — including law, property, social morality, government, constitutions and so on — must be made to conform to general principles of reason. Only then will individuals freely choose to accept and support these institutions. Only then will law, morality and government cease to be arbitrary rules and powers which free agents must be compelled to obey. Only then will human beings be free and yet fully reconciled with the world in which they live.

This notion of making all social institutions conform to general principles of reason has about it the ring of the Enlightenment. To subject everything to the clear cold light of reason, rejecting all that has its basis in superstition or hereditary privilege, was the doctrine of French thinkers of the eighteenth century like Voltaire and Diderot. The Enlightenment and its sequel, the French Revolution, are indeed the next — and almost the last — events in Hegel's account of world history; but

Hegel's attitude towards it is not quite what his remarks about the essence of the Reformation might lead one to expect.

Hegel accepts the view that the French Revolution was the result of the criticisms of the existing order made by French philosophers. France before the Revolution had a nobility without real power, but with a confused mass of privileges which had no rational basis. Against this utterly irrational state of affairs the philosophers' conception of the Rights of Man asserted itself, and triumphed. Hegel leaves us in no doubt as to his view of the significance of this event.

> Never since the sun has stood in the firmament and the planets revolved around it had it been perceived that man's existence centres in his head, i.e. in thought, inspired by which he builds up the world of reality ... not until now had man advanced to the recognition of the principle that thought ought to govern spiritual reality. This was accordingly a glorious mental dawn. All thinking beings shared in the jubilation of this epoch.

Yet the immediate result of this 'glorious mental dawn' was the Revolutionary Terror, a form of tyranny which exercised its power without legal formalities and inflicted as its punishment the quick death of the guillotine. What had gone wrong? The mistake was to attempt to put into practice purely abstract philosophical principles, without regard to the disposition of the people. This attempt was based upon a misunderstanding of the role of reason, which must not be applied in isolation from the existing community and the people that make it up.

The French Revolution itself was thus a failure. Its world-historical significance, however, lies in the principles it passed on to other nations, and particularly to Germany. The short-lived victories of Napoleon were sufficient to bring about within Germany a code of rights, to establish freedom of the person and freedom of property, to open the offices of the State to the most talented citizens and to abolish feudal obligations. The monarch remains as the apex of government and his personal decision is final; yet because of the firmly established laws and settled organisation of the State, what is left to the personal decision of the monarch is, says Hegel, 'in point of substance, no great matter'.

Hegel's account of world history has now reached his own times, and so it comes to an end. He concludes by repeating (in slightly different words) the theme he introduced at the start of it all — 'the history of the world is nothing but the development of the idea of freedom' — and suggesting that the progress of the idea of freedom has now reached its consummation. What was required was both that individuals should govern themselves according to their own conscience and convictions, and also that the objective world, that is the real world with all its social and political institutions, should be rationally organised. It would not be sufficient to have individuals governing themselves according to their own conscience and convictions. This would be only 'subjective freedom'. As long as the objective world was not rationally organised, individuals acting in accordance with their own conscience would come into conflict with its law and morality. Existing law and morality would therefore be something opposed to them, and a limit upon their freedom. Once the objective world is rationally organised, on the other hand, individuals following their consciences will freely choose to act in accordance with the law and morality of the objective world. Then freedom will exist on both the subjective and the objective level. There will be no restrictions on freedom, for there will be perfect harmony between the free choices of individuals and the needs of society as a whole. The idea of freedom will have become a reality and the history of the world will have achieved its goal.

This is a climactic ending indeed; but it leaves an obvious question dangling. What would a rational organisation of morality, law and other social institutions be like? What is a truly rational State? In the *Philosophy of History* Hegel has very little to say on this subject. His rosy description of the Germany of his own day, coupled with his statement that the progress of the idea of freedom has now reached its consummation, can only mean that he believes his own country, in his own times, to have achieved the status of a rationally organised society. He refrains from saying this explicitly, though, and his description of modern Germany is too brief to allow us to see clearly why the particular arrangements he describes should be more rational than all previous forms of government.

The reason for this brevity may simply be that the *Philosophy of History* was written as a course of lectures, and university lecturers, as we all know, frequently find themselves short of time near the end of the course; but it is equally possible that Hegel deliberately said little about this subject in the *Philosophy of History*, because it is the chief focus of his *Philosophy of Right*. It is to this work that we must turn for a more complete picture of what Hegel takes to be a rationally organised and hence genuinely free community.

3 Freedom and community

A puzzle

We have seen that Hegel believes all the events of the past to have been leading up to the goal of freedom. At the conclusion of the *Philosophy of History* there was an indication that this goal might have been reached; but Hegel provided few indications why Prussia (or any of the other German States existing at that time) should be regarded as the glorious result for which three thousand years of world history had been striving. When Hegel gave his lectures on the philosophy of history, Prussia's period of liberal reform under von Stein and von Hardenberg was over. Prussia was dominated by the King and a few other powerful families. It lacked a parliament of any importance, denied the overwhelming majority of its citizens any say in the running of the State, and imposed a strict censorship. How could Hegel have regarded such a society as the pinnacle of human freedom? Is it any wonder that the German philosopher Arthur Schopenhauer should have said, with Hegel in mind: 'Governments make of philosophy a means of serving their State interests, and scholars make of it a trade'? Or that Karl Popper should believe that Hegel had one aim, 'to fight against the open society, and thus to serve his employer, Frederick William of Prussia'?

In this chapter I shall try to explain Hegel's concept of freedom. If I succeed, I will have shown that whatever his motivation, Hegel's thinking on this subject has to be taken seriously because it cuts deeply into assumptions we frequently make when we say that one society is free and another is not.

We have seen that in the introduction to the *Philosophy of History* Hegel says that world history is nothing but the progress of consciousness of freedom. He adds, a few lines further on, that this term 'freedom' is 'an indefinite, and incalculably ambiguous term ... liable to an infinity of misunderstandings, confusions and errors'. Unfortunately he declines to give a further definition, saying that instead the essential nature of freedom 'is to be displayed' in the process of interpreting the history of the world. This is not entirely satisfactory. Our examination of the *Philosophy of History* may have given us a glimmering of what Hegel takes freedom to be; but if so, it is a glimmering that urgently requires the further illumination of Hegel's more explicit comments in the *Philosophy of Right*.

First, a word about the title. To an English-speaking reader, 'Philosophy of Right' suggests a work about right and wrong, in other words a study of ethics. Ethics does figure prominently in Hegel's *Philosophy of Right*, but its subject is closer to political philosophy. The German word in Hegel's title which is translated as 'Right' is *Recht*. This can mean 'right', but has wider associations, including that of 'law', in the sense in which we refer to 'the Law' as a whole rather than to one particular law. So the *Philosophy of Right* expresses Hegel's philosophical ideas about ethics, jurisprudence, society and the state. Since freedom is always central to Hegel's concerns, the *Philosophy of Right* contains Hegel's most detailed discussion of freedom in the social and political sphere. Naturally, it contains discussions of other topics as well, but I shall pass over them in the interest of pursuing the crucial concept of freedom.

Abstract freedom

It will be best to begin with something familiar. Consider what might be called the classical liberal conception of freedom. Liberals generally see freedom as the absence of restrictions. I am free if others do not interfere with me and do not force me to do what I do not want to do. I am free when I can do as I please. I am free when I am left alone. This is the concept of freedom that Isaiah Berlin, in his celebrated essay 'Two Concepts of Liberty', called 'negative freedom'.

Hegel was familiar with this concept of freedom but, unlike Berlin and many other contemporary liberals and libertarians who regard it as the most desirable form of freedom, he refers to it as formal or abstract freedom, meaning that it has the form of freedom, but not the substance. He writes; 'If we hear it said that the definition of freedom is ability to do what we please, such an idea can only be taken to reveal an utter immaturity of thought, for it contains not even an inkling of the absolutely

free will, of right, ethical life, and so forth.' Hegel's objection
to this notion of freedom is that it takes the choices of the individual as the basis from which freedom must begin – how and
why these choices are made is a question that those who hold
this conception of freedom do not ask. Hegel does ask it, and
his answer is that the individual choice, considered in isolation
from everything else, is the outcome of arbitrary circumstances.
Hence it is not genuinely free.

This seems high-handed. How dare Hegel tell us that our
choices are arbitrary – while his, presumably, are genuinely
free? Is this anything more than a blatant attempt to impose his
values on us?

Maybe. But we may become a little more sympathetic to what
Hegel is trying to say if we consider an analogous contemporary
debate. Some economists believe that the proper test of how well
an economic system works is the extent to which it enables
people to satisfy their preferences. These economists take individual preferences as the basis from which assessment must
begin. They do not ask how these preferences come about. To
select among preferences and give some preferences more weight
than others (apart from the differing weights given to their
preferences by the individuals who hold them) would be, these
economists say, a blatant attempt to impose one's own values on
others by denying them the capacity to decide what they really
want out of life.

I shall call these economists 'liberal economists'. The liberal
economists have their critics, whom I shall call 'radical economists'. The radical economists ask some questions about how
individual preferences are formed before they agree to take such
preferences as the sole basis for judging how well an economic
system works. They bring up examples of the following kind:
suppose that at a certain time people in our society take the
normal human body odours for granted. That humans sweat
and that it is possible to smell a sweaty person are things they
barely notice, and in so far as they do notice them, they do not
consider them unpleasant. Then someone discovers a product
which has the effect of inhibiting sweat and the odour it gives
off. That is an interesting discovery, but, in the society described, interest in the product will be very limited. Our

inventor, however, does not give up easily. He launches a clever advertising campaign designed to make people anxious about whether they sweat more than other people, and whether their friends might find their body odour offensive. His advertising is successful. People develop a preference for using the new product; and because the product is widely available at a price within their means, they can satisfy this preference. From the standpoint of the liberal economists, all this is fine. That the economy works in this way provides them with no basis for rating it less favourably than they otherwise would have. The radical economists think this is manifestly absurd. To avoid such absurdities, they say, economists must face the difficult task of enquiring into the basis of preferences, and must judge economic systems by their ability to satisfy not just any preferences, but those preferences that are based on genuine human needs or contribute to genuine human welfare. The radical economists concede that if we adopt their method, we cannot claim that our assessment is value-free; but they add that no method of assessing an economic system can be value-free. The method of assessment used by the liberal economists simply took the satisfaction of existing preferences as its sole value. A value-judgement is therefore implicit in the use of this method, though disguised under a cloak of objectivity. The liberal economists effectively give their blessing to whatever circumstances happen to influence what people prefer.

There is a clear parallel between this debate and Hegel's debate with those who define freedom as the ability to do what we please. This negative concept of freedom is like the liberal economist's conception of a good economic system: it refuses to ask what influences form the 'pleasings' that we act upon when we are free to do as we please. Those who hold this conception of freedom assert that to ask such a question, and to use the answers as a basis for sorting out genuinely free choices from those that are free only in form and not in substance, would be to write one's own values into the conception of freedom. Hegel's retort, like that of the radical economists, would be that the negative conception of freedom is already based on a value, the value of action based on choice, no matter how that choice is reached or how arbitrary it may be. The negative conception of

freedom, in other words, gives its blessing to whatever circumstances happen to be influencing the way people choose.

If you agree that it is absurd to see no objection to an economic system that artificially creates new preferences so that
some may profit by satisfying them, you must agree that the
radical economists have a point. Admittedly it will be difficult to
sort out the preferences which contribute to genuine human
welfare from those that do not. It may prove impossible to reach
agreement on this. Nevertheless, the difficulty of the task is no
reason for taking all preferences at face value.

If you agree that the radical economists have a point, it is only
a small step to agreeing that Hegel has a point. Indeed, it is
really no step at all; for Hegel anticipated the central point of
the radical economists' position, a point that has been popular-
ised in the twentieth century by J. K. Galbraith, Vance Packard
and a host of other critics of the modern industrial economy.
Here is Hegel, writing at the very infancy of the consumer
society, but perceptive enough to pick up the way it was going:

> What the English call 'comfort' is something inexhaustible
> and illimitable. Others can reveal to you that what you take to
> be comfort at any stage is discomfort, and these discoveries
> never come to an end. Hence the need for greater comfort
> does not exactly arise within you directly; it is suggested to
> you by those who hope to make a profit from its creation.

This remark occurs in a section of the *Philosophy of Right*
that examines what Hegel calls 'The System of Needs'; it follows
hard upon a reference to the great figures in classical liberal
economic theory, Adam Smith, J. B. Say and David Ricardo.
Hegel's criticism of this 'system of needs' shows that the ground
of his opposition to the liberal economic view of society was
essentially that taken by radical economists today. Behind it lies
Hegel's steady historical perspective. He never loses sight of the
fact that our wants and desires are shaped by the society in
which we live, and that this society in turn is a stage in a
historical process. Hence abstract freedom, the freedom to do as
we please, is effectively the freedom to be pushed to and fro by
the social and historical forces of our times.

As a criticism of the negative concept of freedom, Hegel's

view should by now seem reasonable enough. What, however, does he intend to put in its place? We all must live in a particular society at a particular period of history. We will all be shaped by the society and times in which we live. How then can freedom be anything more than the freedom to act as we are led to act by social and historical forces?

Freedom and duty

Some of our desires are the product of our nature – like the desire for food, we were born with them, or like sexual desires, we were born with the potential to develop them. Many of our other desires were formed by our upbringing, our education, the society in which we live, our environment generally. Biological or social as the origins of these desires might be, it is true in either case that we did not choose them. Since we did not choose our desires, we are not free when we act from desire.

This argument is reminiscent of Kant rather than Hegel, but Hegel goes along with it up to a point. Let us follow it a little further. If we are not free when we act from desire, it seems that the only possible path to freedom is to purge oneself of all desires. But what would then be left? Kant's answer is: reason. Motivation to action can come from desires, or from reason. Do away with the desires, and we are left with pure practical reason.

Action based on reason alone – the idea is not easy to grasp. We can talk readily enough of a person's actions being rational or irrational, but we normally do so in relation to the ultimate ends or goals that person has, and these ends will be based on desires. For example, knowing that Mohammed Ali desires to retain his reputation as a great boxer, I may say that it is irrational for him to attempt yet another come-back at the age of thirty-seven; but if I am asked whether I consider it rational of Ali to desire to retain his reputation, what can I say? Only that this kind of desire is too basic to be either rational or ir-rational: it is just a brute fact about the man. Can there be judgements of rationality or irrationality which are not based on basic desires of this kind?

Kant says there can be. When we take away all particular desires, even the most basic ones, we are left with the bare, formal element of rationality, and this bare formal element is the universal form of the moral law itself. This is Kant's famous 'categorical imperative', which he puts thus: 'Act only so that the maxim of your action can be willed as a universal law.'

The most puzzling step in this is the move from bare formal rationality to the idea of something universal. Kant holds – and Hegel obviously agrees – that reason is implicitly universal. If we know that all men are mortal and that Socrates was a man, then a law of reasoning tells us that Socrates was mortal. The law of reasoning that tells us this is a universal law – it holds not just for Greeks or for philosophers or even for Earthlings, but for all rational beings. In practical reasoning – that is, reasoning about what to do – this universal element is often concealed by the fact that we start from particular desires which are anything but universal. Consider this piece of practical reasoning: 'I want to be rich; I can defraud my employer of a million dollars without being detected; therefore I should defraud my employer.' Here the reasoning starts from my desire to be rich. There is nothing universal about this desire. (Don't be misled by the fact that many people desire to be rich; the desire from which I begin this reasoning is the desire that I, Peter Singer, should be rich. Very, very few people share this desire.) Because there is nothing universal about the starting-point of this piece of reasoning, there is nothing universal about its conclusion, which certainly does not hold for all rational beings. If we were to reason about what to do *without* starting from any particular desire, however, there would be nothing to prevent our reasoning from holding for all rational beings. Pure practical reasoning, independently of particular desires, could only embody the universal element in reasoning. It would therefore, Kant contends, take the form prescribed by the categorical imperative.

If Kant is right, the only kind of action that is not the result of our innate or socially conditioned desires is action in accordance with the categorical imperative. Only action in accordance with the categorical imperative, therefore, can be free. Since only free action can have genuine moral worth, the categorical imperative must be not only the supreme imperative of reason, but also the supreme law of morality.

One final point is needed to complete the picture. If my action is free, my motivation for acting in accordance with the categorical imperative cannot be any particular desire I might happen to have. It cannot, therefore, be my desire to go to heaven, or to win the esteem of my friends; nor can it be my benevolent desire to do good to others. My motivation must simply be to act in accord with the universal law of reason and morality, for its own sake. I must do my duty because it is my duty — the Kantian ethic is sometimes summed up in the slogan: 'Duty for duty's sake.' It does indeed follow from what Kant said that we are free when we do our duty for its own sake, and not otherwise.

So we have arrived at the conclusion that freedom consists in doing one's duty. To the modern reader this conclusion is paradoxical. The term 'duty' has come to be associated with obedience to the conventional rules of institutions like the army and the family. When we speak of doing our duty we often mean that we are doing what we would much rather not be doing, but feel ourselves constrained to do by customary rules we are reluctant to defy. 'Duty' in this sense is the very opposite of freedom.

If this is the basis of the paradoxical air of the conclusion that freedom consists in doing our duty, we should put it aside. Kant's conclusion was that freedom consists in doing what we really see as our duty in the broadest sense of the term. To put his point in a way that modern readers might be readier to accept: freedom consists in following one's conscience. This accurately captures Kant's meaning, as long as we remember that 'conscience' here does not mean whatever socially conditioned 'inner voice' I may happen to have; it means a conscience based on a rational acceptance of the categorical imperative as the supreme moral law. Put this way, the conclusion we have reached so far may still stretch credulity, but it should no longer appear paradoxical. Freedom of conscience is, after all, widely recognised as an essential part of what we take freedom to be, even if it is not the whole of it.

It is time to return to Hegel. Much of what I have been describing as a Kantian position is also Hegelian. That we are not free when we act from particular innate or socially conditioned desires; that reason is essentially universal; that freedom is to be found in what is universal — all of this Hegel takes from Kant and makes his own. Moreover in the *Philosophy of History*, as we have seen, Hegel takes the Reformation as the dawning of the new age of freedom, because it proclaims the rights of the individual conscience. Thus Hegel, like Kant, sees a connection between freedom and the development of the individual conscience. Nor does Hegel dissent from the idea that freedom consists in doing one's duty. Duty, he says, appears as a restriction on our natural or arbitrary desires, but the truth is that 'in duty the individual finds his liberation ... from mere natural impulse ... In duty the individual acquires his substantive freedom.' Commenting directly on Kant, Hegel said: 'In doing my duty I am by myself and free. To have emphasised this meaning of duty has constituted the merit of Kant's philosophy and its loftiness of outlook.'

For Hegel, then, doing our duty for its own sake is a notable advance on the negative idea of freedom as doing what we please. Yet Hegel is not satisfied with Kant's position. He sees its positive elements, but he is at the same time one of its most trenchant critics. Part II of the *Philosophy of Right*, entitled 'Morality', is in large part an attack on Kant's ethical theory.

Hegel has two main objections. The first is that Kant's theory never gets down to specifics about what we ought to do. This is not because Kant himself lacked interest in such practical questions, but because his entire theory insists that morality must be based on pure practical reasoning, free from any particular motives. As a result, the theory can yield only the bare, universal form of the moral law; it cannot tell us what our specific duties are. This universal form is, Hegel says, simply a principle of consistency or non-contradiction. If we have no point to start from, it cannot get us anywhere. For example, if we accept the validity of property, theft is inconsistent; but we can deny that property gives rise to any rights and be perfectly consistent thieves. If the directive 'Act so as not to contradict yourself!' is the *only* thing we have to move us to act, we may find ourselves doing nothing at all.

This objection to Kant's categorical imperative will be familiar not only to students of Kant, but also to those who have an interest in contemporary moral philosophy. The importance of the requirement that moral principles be universal in form is still widely insisted upon – for example, by R. M. Hare, author of

Freedom and Reason and *Moral Thinking* – and the objection that this requirement is an empty formalism that tells us nothing is still frequently made. In defence of Kant it has been suggested that we should interpret him as allowing us to start from our desires, but requiring that we act upon them only if we are able to put them into a universal form, that is, to accept them as a suitable basis of action for anyone in a similar situation. Hegel anticipates this interpretation, claiming that any desire can be put into a universal form, and hence, once the introduction of particular desires is allowed, the requirement of universal form is powerless to prevent us justifying whatever immoral conduct takes our fancy.

Hegel's second major objection to Kant is that the Kantian position divides man against himself, locks reason into an eternal conflict with desire, and denies the natural side of man any right to satisfaction. Our natural desires are merely something to be suppressed, and Kant gives to reason the arduous, if not impossible, task of suppressing them. In this objection, as we have seen, Hegel was following the lead given by Schiller in his *Lectures on the Aesthetic Education of Man*; but Hegel made his own use of Schiller's criticism.

We can put the point in terms of another familiar problem of modern ethics. For Hegel the second major objection to Kant's ethics is that it offers no solution to the opposition between morality and self-interest. Kant leaves unanswered, and for ever unanswerable, the question: 'Why should I be moral?' We are told that we should do our duty for its own sake, and that to ask for any other reason is to depart from the pure and free motivation morality demands; but this is no answer at all, just a refusal to allow the question to be raised.

In his *Aesthetic Education of Man*, Schiller had pointed back to a time when the question had simply not arisen, when morality had not been split off into something separate from customary ideals of the good life, when there was no Kantian conception of duty. Hegel saw that once the question had been asked, a return to customary morality was impossible. In any case, Hegel regarded the Kantian conception of duty as an advance that is not to be regretted, for it helps to make modern man free in a way the Greeks, embedded in their narrow customary horizons, never could be. What Hegel sought to do was to answer the question in a way that united the natural satisfaction of the Greek form of life with the free conscience of the Kantian idea of morality. His answer would at the same time provide a remedy for the other chief defect of the Kantian theory, its total lack of content.

The organic community

Hegel finds the unity of individual satisfaction and freedom in conformity to the social ethos of an organic community. What sort of community did he have in mind?

Towards the end of the nineteenth century Hegel's idea of an organic community was adopted by the British philosopher F. H. Bradley, who may not have equalled Hegel as an original thinker, but definitely surpassed him as a prose stylist. I shall therefore let Bradley's presentation of the basis of the harmony between private interest and communal values speak for Hegel. Bradley is describing the development of the child growing up in a community:

> The child ... is born ... into a living world ... He does not even think of his separate self; he grows with his world, his mind fills and orders itself; and when he can separate himself from that world, and know himself apart from it, then by that time his self, the object of his self-consciousness, is penetrated, infected, characterized by the existence of others. Its content implies in every fibre relations of community. He learns, or already perhaps has learnt, to speak, and here he appropriates the common heritage of his race, the tongue that he makes his own is his country's language, it is ... the same that others speak, and it carries into his mind the ideas and sentiments of the race ... and stamps them in indelibly. He grows up in an atmosphere of example and general custom ... The soul within him is saturated, is filled, is qualified by, it has assimilated, has got its substance, has built itself up from, it *is* one and the same life with the universal life, and if he turns against this he turns against himself.

Bradley's point – and Hegel's – is that because our needs and desires are shaped by society, an organic community fosters those desires that most benefit the community. Moreover it so imbues its members with the sense that their own identity consists in being a part of the community that they will no more think of going off in pursuit of their own private interests than one part of the organism that is my body — say, my left arm — would think of hiving off from my shoulder to find something better to do than stuff my mouth with food. Nor should we forget that the relationship between an organism and its parts is reciprocal. I need my left arm and my left arm needs me. The organic community will no more disregard the interests of its members than I would disregard an injury to my left arm.

If we can accept this organic model of a community, we shall grant that it would end the ancient conflict between the interests of the individual and the interests of the community; but how does it preserve freedom? Does it not display mere small-minded conformity to custom? Where does it differ from the Greek communities which Hegel regarded as lacking the essential principle of human freedom brought forward in the Reformation and captured, if one-sidedly, in Kant's notion of duty?

The citizens of Hegel's community differ from those of the Greek city-states precisely because they belong to a different historical era and have the achievements of Rome, Christianity and the Reformation as part of their intellectual heritage. They are aware of their capacity for freedom and their ability to make their own decisions in accordance with their conscience. A customary morality, which demands conformity to its rules simply because it is the custom to conform to them, cannot command the obedience of free thinking beings. (We saw how the questioning of Socrates was a mortal threat to the basis of the Athenian community.) Free thinking beings can only give their allegiance to institutions that they recognise as conforming to rational principles. Therefore the modern organic community, unlike the ancient ones, must be based on principles of reason.

In the *Philosophy of History* we saw what happened when people first ventured to strike down irrational institutions and build a new State based on purely rational principles. The leaders of the French Revolution understood reason in a purely abstract and universal sense which would not tolerate the natural dispositions of the community. The Revolution was the political embodiment of the mistake Kant made in his purely abstract and universal conception of duty, which would not tolerate the natural side of human beings. In keeping with this pure rationalism the monarchy was abolished, and all other degrees of nobility as well. Christianity was replaced by the cult of Reason, and the old system of weights and measures abolished to make way for the more rational metric system. Even the calendar was reformed. The result was the Terror, in which the bare universal comes into conflict with the individual and negates him – or, to put it in less Hegelian terms, the State sees individuals as its enemies and puts them to death.

Disastrous as the failure of the French Revolution was for those who suffered by it, there is a crucial lesson to be learnt from it, namely that to build a State on a truly rational basis we must not raze everything to the ground and attempt to start again completely from scratch. We must search for what is rational in the existing world and allow that rational element to have its fullest expression. In this manner we can build on the reason and virtue that already exists in a community.

Here is a modern parable that may illustrate why Hegel regards the French Revolution as a glorious failure, and what he would have us learn from it. When people first began to live in towns, no one thought of town planning. They just put up their houses, shops and factories wherever seemed most convenient, and the cities grew higgledy-piggledy. Then along came someone who said: 'This is no good! We are not thinking about how we want our towns to look. Our lives are being ruled by chance! We need someone to plan our towns, to make them conform to our ideals of beauty and good living.' So along came the town planners, who bulldozed the old neighbourhoods and erected streamlined high-rise apartment buildings, surrounded by swathes of green lawns. Roads were widened and straightened, shopping centres were put up in the midst of generous parking areas, and factories were carefully isolated from residential zones. Then the town planners sat back and waited for the people to thank them. But the people complained that from their high-rise apartments they could not watch their children as they played on the lawns ten floors below. They complained that they missed the local corner shops, and that it was too far to walk across all those green lawns and parking spaces to the shopping centres. They complained that since everyone now had to drive to work, even those new wide straight roads were choked with traffic. Worst of all, they complained that, now no one was walking, the streets had become unsafe and those lovely green lawns were dangerous to cross after dark. So the old town planners were fired, and a new generation of town planners grew up, who had learnt from the mistakes of their predecessors. The first thing the new town planners did was to put a stop to the demolition of old neighbourhoods. Instead they began to notice the positive features of the old, unplanned towns. They admired the varied vistas of the narrow, crooked streets, and noticed how convenient it was to have shops and residences and even small factories mixed up together. They remarked on how these streets kept traffic to a minimum, encouraged people to walk, and made the town centre both lively and safe. Not that their admiration for the old unplanned towns was totally unreserved; there were a few things that needed to be tidied up, some particularly offensive industries were moved away from where people lived, and many old buildings had to be restored or else replaced with buildings in keeping with the surroundings. What the new town planners had discovered, however, was that the old cities *worked*; and it was this that had to be preserved, whatever tinkering might still be desirable.

The old, unplanned cities are like the ancient communities that grew up with custom as their basis; the first town planners resemble the French revolutionaries in their fervour to impose rationality on reality; while the second generation of planners are the true Hegelians, made wiser by the past and ready to find rationality in a world that is the result of practical adaptation rather than deliberate planning.

Now we can see why the free citizens of the modern era give their allegiance to a community which, at first glance, does not differ greatly from the custom-based communities of the ancient world. These free citizens understand the rational principles on which their community is based, and so they freely choose to serve it.

There are, of course, some differences between the modern

rational community and the communities of ancient Greece. Because the modern era knows that all human beings are free, slavery has been abolished. Without slavery, Hegel believes, the time-consuming form of democracy practised in Athens is unworkable. Nor does Hegel think much of representative democracy with universal suffrage, partly because he thinks individuals cannot be represented (he says only 'the essential spheres of society and its large-scale interests' are suitable for representation) and partly because with universal suffrage each individual vote has so little significance that there is widespread apathy, and power falls into the hands of a small caucus of particular interests.

The rational community is, Hegel says, a constitutional monarchy. A monarchy is required because somewhere there must be the power of ultimate decision, and in a free community this power should be expressed by the free decision of a person. (Compare the Greek communities, which often consulted an oracle — a force external to the community — for the final resolution of difficult issues.) On the other hand, Hegel says, if the constitution is stable the monarch often has nothing to do but sign his name. Hence his personal make-up is unimportant, and his sovereignty is not the capricious rule of an oriental despot. The other elements of the constitutional monarchy are the executive and the legislature. The executive consists of civil servants. The only objective qualification for office is proof of ability; but where there are several eligible candidates and their relative abilities cannot be determined with precision, a subjective condition enters which it is the task of the monarch to decide. Hence the monarch retains the right to appoint the executive. The legislature, in keeping with Hegel's ideas of representation, has two houses of parliament, the upper consisting of the landed class and the lower of the business class. It is, however, 'large-scale interests' such as corporations and professional guilds that are represented in the lower house, not individual citizens as such.

I have dealt swiftly with these details of Hegel's rational community because to readers living in the twentieth century his preferences can only seem quaint, and his arguments for them have often — though not always — been shown by subsequent experience to be erroneous. So far as Hegel's conception of freedom is concerned, the particular institutional arrangements he prefers are not crucial. It should by now be clear that Hegel is not talking about freedom in the political sense in which popular sovereignty is an essential element of a free society. He is interested in freedom in a deeper, more metaphysical sense. Hegel's concern is with freedom in the sense in which we are free when we are able to choose without being coerced either by other human beings or by our natural desires, or by social circumstances. As we have seen, Hegel believes such freedom can exist only when we choose rationally, and we choose rationally only when we choose in accordance with universal principles. If these choices are to bring us the satisfaction which is our due, the universal principles must be embodied in an organic community organised along rational lines. In such a community individual interests and the interests of the whole are in harmony. In choosing to do my duty I choose freely because I choose rationally, and I achieve my own fulfilment in serving the objective form of the universal, namely the State. Moreover — and here is the remedy for the second great defect in Kantian ethics — because the universal law is embodied in the concrete institutions of the State, it ceases to be abstract and empty. It prescribes to me the specific duties of my station and role in the community.

We may well reject Hegel's description of a rationally organised community. Our rejection will not affect the validity of his conception of freedom. Hegel was seeking to describe a community in which individual interests and the interests of the whole are in harmony. If he failed, others can continue the search. If none succeeds, if we finally accept that no one ever will succeed, we will have to acknowledge that freedom, in Hegel's sense, cannot exist. Even that would not invalidate Hegel's claim to have described the only genuine form of freedom, and this form of freedom could still serve as an ideal.

Liberal? Conservative? Totalitarian?

We began this chapter with a puzzle. How could Hegel, who stresses freedom to the point of making it the goal of history, suggest that freedom had been achieved in the autocratic

German society of his own time? Was he a servile toady who wished to endear himself to his rulers by twisting the meaning of the term into its very opposite? Worse still, was he the intellectual grandfather of the type of totalitarian State that emerged in Germany a hundred years after his death?

The first step to clearing up this puzzle is to ask a question of fact: Is the ideally rational State that Hegel describes merely a description of the Prussian State at the time he was writing? It is not. There are strong similarities, but there are also significant differences. I shall mention four. Probably the most important is that Hegel's constitutional monarch ideally had little to do except sign his name, whereas Frederick William III of Prussia was much more of an absolute monarch than that. A second difference is that there was no functioning parliament at all in Prussia; Hegel's legislature, though relatively powerless, did provide an outlet for the expression of public opinion. Thirdly, Hegel was, if within very definite limits, a supporter of freedom of expression. Admittedly, by today's standards he appears most illiberal on this issue, for he excluded from this freedom anything that amounted to slander, abuse or 'contemptuous caricature' of the government and its ministers. We are not now seeking to judge him by today's standards, however, but to compare his proposals with the state of affairs in Prussia at the time he was writing; and since the *Philosophy of Right* appeared only eighteen months after the strict censorship imposed by the Carlsbad decrees of 1819, Hegel was certainly arguing for greater freedom of speech than was allowed at the time. Fourthly, Hegel advocated trial by jury as a way of involving citizens in the legal process; but there was no right to trial by jury in Prussia at the time.

These differences are sufficient to acquit Hegel of the charge of having drawn up his philosophy entirely in order to please the Prussian monarchy. They do not, however, make Hegel any kind of liberal in the modern sense. His rejection of the right to vote and his restrictions on freedom of speech are enough to show this. His dislike of anything smacking of popular representation went so far that he wrote an essay opposing the English Reform Bill, which when finally passed in 1832 ended notorious inequalities and abuses in the election of members of the House

of Commons (while still excluding the majority of adult males —
let alone females — from the electoral roll).

After what we have seen of Hegel's ideas of freedom, however, this should come as no surprise. Hegel would have thought
that popular suffrage would amount to people voting in accordance with their material interests or with the capricious and even
whimsical likes and dislikes they may form for one candidate
rather than another. Had he been able to witness an election in a
modern democracy, he would not have had to change his mind.
Those who defend democracy today could scarcely disagree
with Hegel over the manner in which most voters decide whom
to favour with their votes; they would differ with Hegel in
regarding the elections as an essential element in a free society,
no matter how impulsive or arbitrary the majority of the electors
may be. Hegel would have emphatically rejected this, on the
grounds that an impulsive or arbitrary choice is not a free act.
We are free only when our choice is based on reason. To make
the entire direction of the State dependent on such arbitrary
choices would, in his view, amount to handing over the destiny
of the community to chance.

Does this mean that Hegel is indeed a defender of the totalitarian State? This is Karl Popper's view, in his widely read *The
Open Society and Its Enemies*, and he backs up the claim with
quotations bound to raise the hackles of any modern liberal
reader. Here are some examples: 'The State is the Divine Idea as
it exists on earth ... We must therefore worship the State as the
manifestation of the Divine on earth ... The State is the march
of God through the world ... The State ... exists for its own
sake.' These quotations are, Popper thinks, enough to show
Hegel's insistence upon 'the absolute moral authority of the
state, which overrules all personal morality, all conscience', and
to give Hegel an important role in the development of modern
totalitarianism.

Hegel's emphasis on rationality as the essential element in
freedom lends further credence to this reading. For who is to
decide what is rational? Armed with the doctrine that only
rational choices are free, any ruler can justify the suppression of
all opposed to his own rational plans for the future of the State.
For if his plans are rational, those who oppose them must be

motivated not by reason but by selfish desires or irrational whims. Their choices, not being rationally based, cannot be free. To suppress their newspapers and leaflets is thus not to restrict free speech, to arrest their leaders is not to interfere with their freedom of action, and to close down their churches and set up new, more rational forms of worship does not interfere with their freedom of religion. Only when these poor misguided people are led by these methods to appreciate the rationality of their leader's plans will they be truly free! If this is Hegel's concept of freedom, did ever a philosopher provide a better example of the Orwellian double-speak that Hitler and Stalin used so effectively to implement their totalitarian designs?

Popper's case is not as strong as it seems. First, his quotations nearly all come not from Hegel's own writings, but from notes of his lectures taken by students and published only after his death, by an editor who explained in his preface that he had done a certain amount of rewriting. Second, at least one of these resonant utterances is a mistranslation. Where Popper quotes 'The State is the march of God through the world', a more accurate translation would be: 'It is the way of God with the world, that the State exists.' This amounts to no more than the claim that the existence of States is in some sense part of a divine plan. Third, for Hegel 'State' does not mean simply 'the government' but refers to all social life. Thus he is not glorifying the government against the people, but referring to the community as a whole. Fourth, these quotations need to be balanced by others, for Hegel frequently presents one aspect of a subject in an extreme form before balancing it against another. Thus Hegel's remarks on the State follow upon earlier passages in which he says: 'the right of subjective freedom is the pivot and centre of the difference between antiquity and modern times' and goes on to say that this right 'in its infinity' has become 'the universal effective principle' of the new form of civilisation. Later, we find him saying: 'What is of the utmost importance is that the law of reason should be shot through and through by the law of particular freedom ...'. Moreover Hegel insists that, 'in view of the right of self-consciousness', laws can have no binding force unless they are universally known. To hang the laws so high that no citizen can read them, as Dionysius the Tyrant is said to have done, or to bury them in learned tomes no ordinary citizen can read, is injustice. Along similar lines is Hegel's searing attack on the reactionary writer von Haller, who defended a doctrine of 'might makes right' that would have suited Hitler well. Of this author Hegel says: 'The hatred of law, of right made determinate in law, is the shibboleth whereby fanaticism, flabby-mindedness and the hypocrisy of good intentions are clearly and infallibly recognised for what they are, disguise themselves as they may.' So strong a defence of the rule of law is an awkward base from which to construct a totalitarian State, with its secret police and dictatorial power.

That the extravagant language Hegel used to describe the State, and his idea that true freedom is to be found in rational choices, are both wide open to misuse and distortion in the service of totalitarianism is undeniable; but that it *is* a misuse is equally undeniable. We have seen enough of his views about constitutional monarchy, freedom of expression, the rule of law, and trial by jury to make this plain. The problem is that Hegel was serious about reason, to an extent that few of us are now. When someone tells us how the affairs of the State can most rationally be conducted, we take him to be expressing his personal preferences. Others, we assume, will have different preferences and as for what is most 'rational', well, since none of us can really tell, we may as well forget about it and settle for what we like best. So when Hegel writes of 'worshipping' the State, or of freedom being realised in a rational State, we are inclined to apply these remarks to whatever type of State takes our fancy — a reading utterly contrary to Hegel's intentions. By a 'rational State' Hegel himself meant something quite objective and quite specific. It had to be a State that individuals really did choose to obey and support, because they genuinely agreed with its principles and truly found their individual satisfaction in being part of it. For Hegel, no rational State could ever deal with its citizens as the Nazi and Stalinist States dealt with theirs. The idea is a contradiction in terms. Similarly, the threat of the interests of the State coming into conflict with and ruthlessly crushing the rights of the individual loses its grip once we realise that in Hegel's rational State the interests of the individual and of the collective are in harmony.

To all this a modern reader will probably react with a 'Yes, but ...'. 'Yes' to indicate that Hegel was not himself advocating totalitarianism; 'but' to suggest that on this interpretation Hegel was extraordinarily optimistic about the possibilities of harmony between humans, and even more extraordinarily at odds with reality if he believed that the harmony would exist in the kind of State he described.

The latter criticism I believe to be unanswerable. If Hegel's remarks about the State are to be defensible, the rational State he has in mind must be very different from any State that existed in his day (or has existed since, for that matter). Yet the State he described, while it may have differed *significantly*, certainly did not differ *radically* from States existing in his own day. The most likely explanation is that Hegel was too conservative, or else too cautious, to advocate a radical departure from the political system under which he lived and taught. To say that Hegel's 'one aim' was to please the King of Prussia is clearly wrong; but it may be fair to say that in order to avoid the wrath of the King of Prussia (and of all the other German rulers) Hegel muted the radical thrust of his underlying philosophical theory.

There is, however, one more thing that needs to be said about Hegel's vision of harmony between humans. His political philosophy is only a part of a much larger philosophical system, in which unity between individual human beings has a metaphysical basis. In the last two chapters we have given the historical and political sides of Hegel's thought more than their fair allocation of space, considering their place in Hegel's work as a whole, and so it is in any case time to move on to the larger philosophical system. We shall soon see that to turn to the other side of Hegel's thought is equally desirable for a deeper understanding of both his philosophy of history and his political philosophy.

4 The odyssey of mind

Mind or spirit?

It is time to confess: I have been cheating. My account of Hegel's philosophy so far has carefully omitted all mention of something that Hegel himself refers to repeatedly and regards as crucial: the idea of *Geist*. So crucial is this idea that Hegel actually says that the whole object of the *Philosophy of History* is to become acquainted with *Geist* in its guiding role in history. Without some knowledge of this idea, therefore, one can have only a partial grasp of Hegel's view of history. In the *Philosophy of Right*, too, the concept of *Geist* is never far away. Hegel refers to the State, for instance, as 'objectified *Geist*'. So the preceding chapters were deliberately misleading; my only excuse is that I misled in a good cause, the cause of easing the reader gently into the strange and often obscure world of Hegel's ideas.

For the English-speaking reader, the difficulties of Hegel's concept of *Geist* begin with its translation. In German the word is common enough, but it has two distinct, though related meanings. It is the standard word used to mean 'mind', in the sense in which our mind is distinct from our body. For example, 'mental illness' is *Geisteskrankheit* – literally, 'mind-sickness'. *Geist* can, however, also mean 'spirit' in the varied senses of that English word. Thus 'the spirit of the times' is *der Zeitgeist*, while the third element of the Christian Trinity of Father, Son and Holy Ghost (or Holy Spirit) is *der Heilige Geist*. The translator's task is made doubly difficult by the fact that in some passages Hegel seems to use the word much as we would use 'mind', in other contexts he uses it as we would use 'spirit', and in others still his usage has elements of both meanings.

In this impossible situation, the translator has three options: to use 'mind' throughout; to use 'spirit' throughout; or to use whichever seems most appropriate in the context. I have rejected the third option, because it is obviously important to Hegel that what he calls *Geist* is one and the same thing, notwithstanding the different aspects of it that emerge in his various writings. When I began work on this book, my presumption was that I would use 'spirit', for this has been the choice of virtually all the recent translators of Hegel. Yet as I began to get more deeply into the attempt to present Hegel in a form that would be understandable to readers who are not already Hegel scholars, I became convinced that to use 'spirit' is to prejudge, for the English-speaking reader, the whole question of what *Geist* really means for Hegel. In English, apart from special usages like 'spirit of the age' and 'team spirit', the word 'spirit' has an inescapably religious or mystical flavour. A spirit taps out the message on the Ouija board, or haunts the deserted Gothic mansion. A spirit is a ghostly, disembodied being, the sort of thing you believe in if you are a bit superstitious, but not if you take a cool, clear scientific view of the world.

Now it may be that at some point in our examination of Hegel we shall have to say that his philosophy is based on this somewhat superstitious view of the world, and his concept of *Geist* is intended to refer to just such a ghostly, disembodied being. We must not, however, assume this from the start. Hegel is a philosopher working in the Western philosophical tradition. Philosophers in this tradition have always been much concerned with the nature of mind, or consciousness, and its relation to the physical world. Descartes began the modern philosophical era by asking what he could know with complete certainty; and he answered by saying that while he might be dreaming, or deceived by an evil demon and hence mistaken in almost all his beliefs, the one thing he could know with certainty is: 'I think, therefore I exist.' I cannot be deceived about that, for to be deceived, I must still exist. What, though, is this 'I'? It is not my physical body – about that I could be deceived. The 'I' that I know with certainty is simply a thing that thinks: in other words, a mind. From this argument arose the central preoccupations of subsequent Western philosophy. How are my thoughts and feelings connected to my body? Are there both mental objects, such as thoughts, and material objects, such as bodies? If so, in what way can two such different kinds of thing interact? My brain is a material thing; how can matter be conscious? This nest of issues is known among philosophers as 'the mind–

body problem'. Another set of issues, also traceable to Descartes, focuses on problems of knowledge: How can we know what the world is like? Can we be sure that our thoughts are in any way a reflection of some 'real' world that is 'out there', as we tend to assume? If all my conscious experiences, including the sensations of colour and shape and texture that I rely upon for simple beliefs like that in the existence of the sheet of paper in front of me now, are always in my mind, how can I ever know anything at all of the world outside my own consciousness?

The point of this digression into the problems of the Western philosophical tradition is simply this: it is entirely to be expected that a philosopher like Hegel should write about mind. That he does so should not suggest that he believes in the existence of disembodied spirits or of anything else in which you and I, cool, clear-thinking adherents of the scientific world-view that we may be, do not also believe. Therefore we should at least start our discussion of what Hegel is saying by taking his references to *Geist* not as talk about some peculiar mystical being, but as a contribution to the long-standing philosophical debate about the nature of mind. Accordingly in this book I return to the practice of an earlier generation of translators of Hegel and render *Geist* as 'mind'. We shall see as we go along in just what sense of that word Hegel's concept is to be understood.

The task of the Phenomenology

That my presentation of Hegel's views up to this point has been seriously incomplete can be seen by returning to a question I brushed aside early in the discussion of Hegel's philosophy of history. *Why* is the history of the world nothing but the progress of the consciousness of freedom? The question cries out for an answer. Hegel explicitly denies – and it would in any case be quite out of keeping with his whole line of thought – that the direction of history is some kind of fortunate accident. Hegel asserts that what happens in history happens *necessarily*. What does this mean? How can it be true? Hegel's answer is that history is nothing but the progress of the consciousness of freedom because history is the development of mind. In the *Philosophy of History* Hegel did not set out to explain this notion, because he had already published a very long and very dense volume intended to demonstrate the necessity of mind developing as it does. That volume is *The Phenomenology of Mind*. Karl Marx called it 'the true birthplace and secret of Hegel's philosophy'. Others, defeated by its 750 pages of bewildering and tortuous prose, have been content to let whatever secrets it might contain rest undisturbed. No account of Hegel, however, can decently overlook it.

The obvious place to start is with the title. The *Oxford English Dictionary* tells us that 'phenomenology' means 'the science of phenomena, as distinct from that of being'. That is all very well if we are familiar with the distinction between 'phenomena' and 'being'. For those that are not, the same dictionary obligingly tells us that 'phenomenon' means, in its philosophical use, 'that of which the senses or the mind directly takes note; an immediate object of perception (as distinguished from substance, or a thing in itself)'. The distinction being made here can be illustrated by considering the difference between the moon as it appears in my vision, and the moon as it really is. In my vision it appeared last night as a silvery crescent no bigger than a tennis-ball; it really is, of course, a sphere of rock with a diameter of several thousand kilometres. The silvery crescent is the phenomenon. Phenomenology, then, is the study of the way in which things appear to us.

If phenomenology is the study of the way in which things appear to us, a 'phenomenology of mind', we might guess, will be a study of the way in which mind appears to us. Such a guess would be correct, but there is a characteristically Hegelian twist to add. When we study how our mind appears to us, we can only be studying how it appears to our minds. Thus a phenomenology of mind is really a study of how mind appears to itself. Accordingly, Hegel's *Phenomenology of Mind* traces different forms of consciousness, viewing each one from inside, as it were, and showing how more limited forms of consciousness necessarily developed into more adequate ones. Hegel himself describes his project as 'the exposition of knowledge as a phenomenon' because he sees the development of consciousness as a development toward forms of consciousness that more fully grasp reality, culminating in 'absolute knowledge'.

In his introduction to the *Phenomenology*, Hegel explains why he believes it necessary to carry out this kind of study. He begins with the problem of knowledge. The aim of philosophy, he says, is the 'actual knowledge of what truly is' or, as he somewhat mysteriously characterises it, 'the absolute'. Before we start to pronounce upon 'what truly is', however, hadn't we better pause to reflect upon knowledge itself, that is, on how we come to know reality? In our attempts to gain knowledge we are attempting to grasp reality. Hence knowledge, Hegel says, is often likened to an instrument by which we grasp truth; if our instrument is faulty we may end up holding nothing but error.

So we begin with an enquiry into knowing. Immediately we are beset by sceptical worries. If trying to know reality is like using some kind of instrument for grasping reality, isn't there a danger that applying our instrument to reality will alter it, so that we grasp something very different from undisturbed reality? (Compare the way modern physicists find it impossible to pin down the speed and location of subatomic particles, because whatever instrument they use to observe them will also interfere with them.) Even if we abandon the 'instrument' metaphor, Hegel says, and regard knowledge as a more passive medium through which we observe reality, we are still observing reality-through-the-medium, not reality itself.

If an instrument or a medium through which we are looking has a distorting effect, one way of coming to know the true state of affairs is to discover the nature of the distortion and subtract the difference it makes. For example, if I look at a stick half in the water and half out, the part in the water appears bent. Is the stick really bent? I can calculate this if I know the law of refraction and thus the difference that looking at it through water makes. Subtracting this difference, I will discover what the stick is really like. Can we perhaps do the same with the distorting effect of the instrument or medium of knowledge, and thus come to know reality as it is?

No, Hegel says, this escape from our puzzle is not open to us. Knowing is not like seeing. For in the case of knowing, what is one to subtract? It would be like subtracting not the difference the water makes to the ray of light, but the ray of light itself. Without knowledge we would not know the stick at all; to subtract our act of knowing, therefore, would be to leave us knowing nothing.

So our instrument cannot guarantee us an image of undisturbed reality, nor can we come closer to reality by making allowances for the disturbance caused by our instrument. Should we therefore embrace the sceptical position that there is nothing we can truly know? But such scepticism, Hegel says, is self-refuting. If we are to doubt everything, why not doubt the claim that we can know nothing? Moreover the sceptical argument we have been considering has its own presuppositions, which it claims to know. It starts with the idea that there is such a thing as reality, and that knowledge is some kind of instrument or medium by which we grasp reality. In so doing, it presupposes a distinction between ourselves and reality, or the absolute. Worse still, it takes for granted that our knowledge and reality are cut off from one another, but at the same time still treats our knowledge as something real, that is, as a part of reality. Thus scepticism will not do either.

Hegel has neatly set up a certain view of knowing, and then shown that it leads into a hole from which we cannot escape, and in which we cannot remain. We must, he now says, abandon all these 'useless ideas and expressions' about knowledge as an instrument or medium, all of which divide knowledge from reality as it is.

In all of this argument there is no mention of any philosopher who has held the view of knowledge that Hegel now says we must reject. To some extent he is criticising assumptions common to the whole school of empiricist philosophers – Locke, Berkeley, Hume and many others. It would, however, have been obvious to all his readers that his main target is Kant. Kant argued that we can never see reality as it is; for we can only comprehend our experiences within the frameworks of space, time and causation. Space, time and causation are not part of reality, but the necessary forms in which we grasp it; therefore we can never know things as they are independently of our knowledge.

In another work, the *Lesser Logic*, Hegel does name his opponent and mounts a similar attack against him (though as if to display his intellectual fertility, he presses home his point with a slightly different argument). The passage is worth quoting, because it concludes with an analogy that suggests the way forward:

> We ought, says Kant, to become acquainted with the instrument, before we undertake the work for which it is to be employed; for if the instrument be insufficient, all our trouble will be spent in vain ... But the examination of knowledge can only be carried out by an act of knowledge. To examine this so-called instrument is the same thing as to know it. But to seek to know before we know is as absurd as the wise resolution of Scholasticus, not to venture into the water until he had learned to swim.

The lesson taught by the folly of Scholasticus is clear. To learn to swim we must plunge boldly into the stream; and to obtain knowledge of reality, we must plunge boldly into the stream of consciousness that is the starting-point of all we know. The only possible approach to knowledge is an examination of consciousness from the inside as it appears to itself – in other words, a phenomenology of mind. We shall not start with sophisticated doubts, but with a simple form of consciousness that takes itself to be genuine knowledge. This simple form of consciousness will, however, prove itself to be something less than genuine knowledge, and so will develop into another form of consciousness; and this in turn will also prove inadequate, and develop into something else, and so the process will continue until we reach true knowledge.

The Phenomenology of Mind is the tracing of this process in detail: as Hegel puts it, 'the detailed history of the process of training and educating consciousness itself up to the level of science'. Part of this training and educating is in fact the development of ideas that has occurred throughout history; thus Hegel's *Phenomenology* is in part an anticipation of the material covered in the *Philosophy of History*. This time, however, the same events are treated in a different manner, for Hegel's aim is to exhibit the process of the development of consciousness as a *necessary* one. Each form of consciousness, in revealing itself to be less than genuine knowledge, leads us to what Hegel calls 'a determinate negation'. This is not the empty scepticism defended by philosophers who find fault with our ordinary methods of knowing; from that empty scepticism there would be no way forward. A determinate negation, on the other hand, is itself something. (Think of the negation sign in mathematics: it produces not zero, but a definite negative number.) The 'something' that is the result of the discovery that a form of consciousness is inadequate, is itself a new form of consciousness, namely, consciousness aware of the inadequacies of the previous form and forced to adopt a different approach in order to surmount them. Thus we shall be compelled to move from one form of consciousness to the next in a restless searching for true knowledge.

The *Phenomenology* will therefore provide an answer to the question raised earlier, as to *why* the history of the world is nothing but the development of the consciousness of the idea of freedom, and why what happens in history happens necessarily. Yet, incredibly, the answer given to this monumental question is merely a by-product of the principal aim of the work, which is to demonstrate the possibility of genuine knowledge, and thus to serve as a foundation for philosophy's aim of providing, as Hegel put it, 'actual knowledge of what truly is'.

The goal of the process to be traced in the *Phenomenology* is true knowledge, or 'the absolute'. How will we know that we have reached it? Will not sceptical doubts still be possible? No, says Hegel, because 'the terminus is at that point where knowledge is no longer compelled to go beyond itself...'. In other words, whereas previously consciousness has been forced to admit that its own knowledge is inadequate, and to strive for more adequate knowledge that is beyond its grasp – to seek to know the 'thing-in-itself' – at the end of the process, reality will no longer be an unknowable 'beyond'. Consciousness will know reality directly, and be at one with it. There will be nothing further to reach for, and the restless compulsion to attain more adequate knowledge will at last be satisfied.

Hegel has set himself an extraordinary task. Beginning with a powerful critique of the approach to knowledge taken by Kant (and not only by Kant, but by all philosophers who start off by assuming a division between one who knows and the thing that is known – which means virtually all philosophers from Plato onwards), Hegel sets out to develop a new method. His method is to trace the development of all the possible forms of consciousness to the final goal of genuine knowledge, which must not be knowledge of the appearance of reality, but knowledge of reality itself. We must now see how he carries out this task.

Knowledge without concepts?

Hegel starts with the most primitive form of consciousness, which he calls 'certainty at the level of sense-experience' or, more briefly, 'sense-certainty'. He has in mind a form of consciousness which does nothing but grasp what is in front of it at any given moment. Sense-certainty simply records the data received by our senses. It is knowledge of the particular thing present to our senses. Sense-certainty makes no attempt to order or classify the raw information obtained by the senses. Thus when this form of consciousness has in front of it what we would describe as a ripe tomato, it cannot describe its experience as a tomato, for that would be to classify what it sees. It cannot even describe the experience as one of seeing something round and red, for these terms too presuppose some form of classification. Sense-certainty is aware only of what is now present to it; as Hegel puts it, it is the certainty of the 'this', or of the 'here' and 'now'.

Sense-certainty seems to have a strong claim to being genuine knowledge, for it is directly aware of the 'this', without imposing on it the distorting filters of a conceptual scheme involving space, time or any other categories. Sense-certainty is simple awareness of the object exactly as it is. Yet, as Hegel shows, the claim that sense-certainty is knowledge does not stand up to further investigation. As soon as sense-certainty attempts to utter its knowledge, it becomes incoherent. What is the 'this'? It can be broken down into the 'here' and the 'now', but these terms cannot convey truth. If, late one night, we are asked what is the 'now', we may reply 'Now it is night-time.' Suppose we write that down – a truth cannot lose anything by being written down, Hegel says, nor by being preserved. So the next day at noon we take out the truth we have written down, only to find that, as Hegel puts it, 'it has turned stale'. Similarly I say 'Here is a tree', but another sense-certainty can just as well say 'Here is a house.'

Hegel's argument seems to be based on a perverse misunderstanding of the language used to convey the knowledge of sense-certainty. Surely it is possible to restate the knowledge of sense-certainty in a manner that is immune to such cheap tricks? Yet the trick is not as easy to get around as one might imagine. From the standpoint of sense-certainty it is not possible to say, for example, 'At midnight it is night' or 'There is a tree in the park.' These utterances presuppose a general ordering of things, including our concepts of time and space.

How then can the knowledge of self-certainty be expressed? Hegel's point is that it cannot be expressed in language at all, because sense-certainty is knowledge of the pure particular, while language always involves bringing something under some more general or universal label. 'Tomato' is a universal term that picks out a whole class of objects, not a single particular object − and the same is true of every other term. Hegel's attack on the truthfulness of 'Now it is night-time' is intended to show that to use terms like 'now', 'here' and 'this' is no way to express knowledge of the pure particular. These terms are also universals, for there is more than one 'now' and more than one 'here'. Thus sense-certainty, in seeking to express its knowledge of the pure particular, has got sucked into the necessity of the universal term.

Hegel believes that he has established the impossibility of knowledge without universal concepts. Two possible objections to his argument are worth brief mention. The first points out an obvious exception to the rule that every term picks out a class of objects rather than a particular object: proper names. 'John D. Rockefeller', 'Rosa Luxemburg', 'The Sydney Opera House' and other proper names do pick out particular objects. Could not sense-certainty describe its experience by giving every 'this' a proper name?

In the *Phenomenology* Hegel ignores the fact that proper names are an exception to his view of language; but we can make a fair guess at what his reply would be, for in his *Logic* he asserts that proper names are meaningless, precisely because they lack reference to anything beyond the name itself, that is, to anything universal. For the particular knowledge of sense-certainty to be expressed by proper names, we can imagine him saying, would be merely to stick meaningless labels on every 'this' of which one was aware. Such labels would convey nothing.

This brings us to the second possible objection, which grants that the knowledge of sense-certainty may be impossible to put into language and convey to others, but contends that it is none the less knowledge. Why should we assume that all knowledge can be put into words? Mystics have often asserted that the truths of mystical experiences are impossible to put into words, and yet are the deepest truths of all. 'A truth cannot lose anything by being written down,' Hegel said; but perhaps this simple claim was the first step down the path away from truth. Should we not have stopped Hegel right there, and insisted on the validity of knowledge too pure for words?

To this objection Hegel must reply, for it threatens the heart of his enterprise. He does not deny that there is something which cannot be reached by language, but he asserts that this is 'nothing else than what is untrue, irrational, something barely and simply believed'. I may well think that I know what I mean, even if I cannot put it into words, but in fact this is not knowledge, it is purely subjective, a personal opinion. Opinion is not knowledge. It can only become knowledge by being brought out into the open.

Hegel makes his point by playing on the multiple meanings of the German 'meinen', to believe or to intend, and its associated noun, 'Meinung', which means 'opinion'. If we disregard this way of doing philosophy by punning, we are left with an assertion rather than an argument. Nevertheless the assertion — that something which is in principle incommunicable cannot possibly be knowledge — is plausible enough.

We can now take stock of our analysis of the claim that this primitive form of consciousness represents genuine knowledge. An attempt was made to state what sort of knowledge could be possessed by a consciousness that does nothing more than grasp what is in front of it at any given moment. The attempt failed, because the truths reached by that form of consciousness proved to be either palpable falsehoods, or something purely personal that can never be expressed. In neither case could these alleged truths be accepted as knowledge.

Thus sense-certainty proved itself inadequate. The result was

achieved, as Hegel promised us in his introduction, from within
– that is, all that was necessary to show the inadequacy of sense-
certainty was to take its claims at face value and try to make
them more precise. Sense-certainty did not succumb to a rival
form of consciousness; it collapsed through its own incoher-
ence. At the same time, and again as we were promised in the
introduction, this outcome was not only a negative result. We
were led to appreciate the impossibility of knowledge of pure
particulars, and thus the necessity of bringing particular sense-
experiences under some form of conceptual scheme, a scheme
that classifies what we experience under a universal aspect, and
so makes it possible to communicate our experience through
language. If we are to achieve knowledge, we cannot passively
experience; we must allow our mind to play a more active role in
ordering the information received by our senses. The next form
of consciousness Hegel examines, therefore, is one in which consciousness actively attempts to create some unity and coherence
out of the raw data of sense-experience.

The emergence of self-consciousness

From the naïve form of consciousness discussed in the preceding
section, Hegel traces the development of consciousness through
two further stages which he calls 'perception' and 'understanding'. In each stage consciousness plays a more active role than it
did in the preceding stage. At the level of perception, consciousness classifies objects according to their universal properties;
this proves inadequate, and so at the level of understanding,
consciousness imposes its own laws on reality. The laws Hegel
has in mind are Newton's laws of physics, and the view of the
universe that came to be based on them. Although these laws are
commonly regarded as a part of reality that Newton and other
scientists have discovered, Hegel sees them as no more than an
extension of the classification by consciousness of the raw data
of sense-experience. Just as bringing these data under universal
categories essential to language made it possible to communicate, so the laws of physics are a way of making the data more
coherent and predictable. The concepts employed in this process
– notions like 'gravity' and 'force' – are not things we see

existing in reality, but constructs made by our understanding to help us grasp reality.

Consciousness at the level of understanding does not see these constructs for what they are; it takes them as objects to be understood. We who trace the process of the development of consciousness can see that consciousness is, in effect, trying to understand its own creations. It has itself for its object. This means that consciousness has reached the point at which it can reflect upon itself. It is latent self-consciousness. With this conclusion Hegel brings the first part of the *Phenomenology* – the part headed 'Consciousness' – to a close. In the following part, under the general title 'Self-consciousness', he drops the direct investigation of the problem of knowledge that provided the focus of the first part, switching his attention to the development of latent self-consciousness into fully explicit self-consciousness. (This is still, of course, part of the development of mind towards the stage of absolute knowledge.)

The desiring mind

Hegel's notion of self-consciousness is important; in different ways, it has influenced both Marxist and existentialist thinkers. Self-consciousness, he maintains, cannot exist in isolation. If consciousness is to form a proper picture of itself, it needs some contrast. It requires an object from which to differentiate itself. I can only become aware of myself if I am also aware of something that is not myself. Self-consciousness is not simply a consciousness contemplating its own navel.

Although self-consciousness needs an object outside itself, this external object is also something foreign to it, and a form of opposition to it. There is therefore a peculiar kind of love–hate relationship between self-consciousness and the external object. This relationship, in the best tradition of love–hate relationships, comes to the surface in the form of desire. To desire something is to wish to possess it – and thus not to destroy it altogether – but also to transform it into something that is yours, and thus to strip it of its foreignness.

The introduction of this notion of desire marks the switch in Hegel's concern from theoretical problems of discovering truth to practical problems of changing the world. We have here a foreshadowing of the 'unity of theory and practice' of which Marxists make so much. Truth is to be obtained not through contemplation alone, but by working on the world and changing it. On Marx's tombstone are engraved the words of his famous Eleventh Thesis on Feuerbach: 'The philosophers have only interpreted the world in various ways; the point, however, is to change it.' Marx certainly had Hegel in mind as one of 'the philosophers', and it is undeniable that Marx wished to change the world far more radically than Hegel did; Hegel could none the less have pointed out that the underlying idea of Marx's words can be found in the *Phenomenology*, at the point where the self-conscious being finds that to realise itself fully it must set about changing the external world and making it its own.

Desire appeared as the expression of the fact that self-consciousness needs an external object, and yet finds itself limited by anything that is outside itself. But to desire something is to be unsatisfied; so desire is – to make a typically Hegelian play on words – an unsatisfactory state for self-consciousness. Worse still, self-consciousness seems doomed to be permanently unsatisfied, for if the object of desire is done away with as an independent object, self-consciousness will have destroyed what it needed for its own existence.

Hegel's solution to this dilemma is to make the object of self-consciousness *another* self-consciousness. In this manner each self-conscious being has another object with which to contrast itself, yet the other 'object' turns out to be not a simple object which must be possessed and thereby 'negated' as an external object, but another self-consciousness which can possess itself, and thereby can do away with itself as an external object.

If this seems obscure, don't worry. It is even more obscure in Hegel's text. One commentator, Ivan Soll, remarks on the 'extreme opacity' of Hegel's argument at this point; another, Richard Norman, deals swiftly with this section, saying: 'since I find large parts of it unintelligible, I shall say little about it'. Hegel's central point is that self-consciousness demands not simply any external object, but another self-consciousness. One way of explaining this is to say that to see oneself, one needs a mirror. To be aware of oneself as a self-conscious being, one needs to be able to observe another self-conscious being, to see what self-consciousness is like. An alternative explanation is that self-consciousness can only develop in a context of social interaction. A child growing up in total isolation from all other self-conscious beings would never develop mentally beyond the level of mere consciousness, for self-consciousness grows out of a social life. Each of these explanations is plausible enough. Unfortunately it is difficult to relate either of them to the words Hegel uses. One or both of them may nevertheless resemble what he had in mind.

Master and slave

We pass now to the most admired section of the entire *Phenomenology*. The two self-consciousnesses are on stage. For ease of exposition, let us refer to self-conscious beings as *persons*. (Hegel, of course, does not deign to make the exposition easier.) Each person, then, needs the other to establish his own awareness of himself. What precisely is it that each requires from the other? Hegel suggests that it is acknowledgement or recognition. To understand his point we need to note that the German word for self-consciousness, '*Selbstbewusstsein*', also has the sense of 'being self-assured' (unlike the English word, which is associated with embarrassment and hesitation). It is this sense of the German word that gives support to Hegel's idea that my self-consciousness is threatened by the existence of another person who fails to acknowledge me as a person. As Richard Norman has suggested, we can take the work of existential psychiatrists like R. D. Laing as an elaboration of this idea. If the worth of one person is systematically denied recognition by all those on whom he or she depends – as can happen in a family in which one member has become a scapegoat for everyone's problems – that person's sense of identity can be utterly destroyed. (The result of this lack of acknowledgement, according to Laing, is schizophrenia.)

If this notion of the need for acknowledgement or recognition is still obscure, consider the analogy of a nation achieving diplomatic recognition. That diplomatic recognition is important to States is obvious from the efforts that some States, like East Germany and China, have made to obtain it – and from the efforts that others have made to prevent them obtaining it. Until a nation has been recognised by others, it is not a full-fledged State. Diplomatic recognition is peculiar in that on the one hand it apparently does no more than recognise something that is already in existence, and yet on the other hand it makes something less than a State into a complete State. The same peculiarity belongs to Hegel's conception of recognition.

The demand for recognition is mutual. One might think, therefore, that people could peacefully recognise each other and be done with it. Instead Hegel tells us that self-consciousness seeks to become pure, and to do this it must show that it is not attached to mere material objects. In fact self-consciousness is doubly attached to material objects: it is attached to its own living body, and to the living body of the other person from whom it requires acknowledgement. The way to prove that one is not attached to either of these material objects is to engage in a life-and-death struggle with the other person: by seeking to kill the other, one shows that one is not dependent on the body of the other, and by risking one's own life, one shows that one is not attached to one's own body either. Hence the initial relationship of the two individuals is not peaceful mutual recognition, but combat.

It is difficult to know what to make of this. Hegel seems to be saying that violent combat is not an accidental occurrence in human affairs, but a necessary element in the process of proving oneself a person. Can he really mean to say, though, that people who have not risked their lives are not really, or fully, persons? Perhaps it would be better — certainly it is more charitable — to regard the process of 'proving' as one that merely makes explicit what was already implicit. (For example, when we prove a theorem, we do not thereby make it true; we only show that it was true all along.) On this interpretation, someone who has never risked his life can still be a person, although his existence as a person has not been demonstrated. Being more charitable still, we might interpret Hegel as holding only that it is necessary, somewhere along the line, that some people stake their lives to prove their independence of their bodies; the proof does not have to be repeated for each person.

To return to the conflict. The original idea was that each individual was intent upon the death of the other. A moment's thought shows, however, that this outcome suits nobody – not the defeated, who will be dead, nor the victor, who will then have destroyed the source of recognition he needs to confirm his sense of himself as a person. So the victor realises that the other person is essential to him, and spares his life; but the original equality of two independent people has been replaced by an unequal situation in which the victor is independent and the loser is dependent. The former is the master, the latter the slave.

In this way Hegel accounts for the division between ruler and ruled. Once again, though, this situation is not stable. The reason Hegel gives for its instability is strikingly original.

At first it seems that the master has everything. He sets the slave to work in the material world, and sits back to enjoy both the subservience of the slave and the fruits of the slave's labours. But consider now the master's need for acknowledgement. He has the acknowledgement of the slave, to be sure, but in the eyes of the master the slave is merely a thing, not an independent consciousness at all. The master has, after all, failed to achieve the acknowledgement he requires.

Nor is the situation of the slave as it first appeared to be. The slave lacks adequate acknowledgement, of course, for to the master he is a mere thing. On the other hand, the slave works on the external world. In contrast to his master, who receives the temporary satisfactions of consumption, the slave shapes and fashions the material objects on which he works. In doing so he makes his own ideas into something permanent, an external object. (For example, if he carves a log of wood into a chair, his conception of a chair, his design and his efforts, remain a part of the world.) Through this process the slave becomes more aware of his own consciousness, for he sees it in front of him as something objective. In labour, even labour under the direction of another, hostile mind, the slave discovers that he has a mind of his own.

Some forty years later Karl Marx developed his own notion of *alienated labour*. Like Hegel, Marx regarded labour as a process in which the worker puts his own thoughts and efforts – in fact all that is best in himself – into the object of his labours. The worker thereby *objectifies* himself, or externalises himself. Marx then made much of a point that is implicit in what Hegel says: if the object of labour is the property of another, especially an alien, hostile other, the worker has lost his own objectified essence. This is what happens to the labour of the slave; but, as Marx insisted, it also happens under capitalism. The chair, shoes, cloth or whatever it is that the worker has produced belong to the capitalist. They enable the capitalist to profit, and thereby to increase his capital and strengthen his dominance over the workers. So the objectified essence of the worker is not merely lost to him; it actually turns into a hostile force that oppresses him. This is alienated labour, the key idea of Marx's early writings and the forerunner of the notion of surplus value which is the basis of the Marxist critique of capitalist economics.

Philosophy and religion

For Marx the solution to the problem of alienated labour was the abolition of private property and of the division of mankind into the rulers and the ruled. Hegel, on the other hand, saw himself as tracing a path that consciousness had already travelled. So there could be no question of leaping off at this point into some future classless society. In fact, it is precisely at this point that the *Phenomenology* becomes more historical, edging closer to the material Hegel was later to deal with more concretely in his *Philosophy of History*. The section on master and slave is followed by a discussion of Stoicism, a philosophical school that became important under the Roman Empire and included among its leading writers both Marcus Aurelius, the Emperor, and Epictetus, a slave. Stoicism therefore bridges the gulf between master and slave. In Stoicism the repressed slave who has come to full self-awareness through work can find a type of freedom; for Stoicism teaches withdrawal from the external world – in which the slave remains a slave – and retreat into one's own consciousness. As Hegel says: 'In thinking I am free, because I am not in another, but remain simply and solely in touch with myself; and the object which for me is my essential reality is ... my own existence.' And again: 'The essence of this consciousness is to be free, on the throne or in chains ...'. The Stoic in chains is still free because chains do not matter to him. He detaches himself from his body and finds his consolation in his mind, where no tyrant can touch him.

The weakness of Stoicism is that thought, cut off from the real world, lacks all determinate content. Its edifying ideas are barren of substance and soon get tedious. Stoicism is then succeeded by another philosophical attitude, scepticism, and from scepticism we progress to what Hegel calls 'the unhappy consciousness', a notion which I shall briefly discuss because of the importance it had to some of Hegel's successors.

'The unhappy consciousness' is clearly a form of consciousness that existed under Christianity. Hegel also refers to it as 'the alienated soul', and this expression provides a better clue to what Hegel has in mind. In the alienated soul, the dualism of master and slave is concentrated into one consciousness, but the two elements are not unified. The unhappy consciousness aspires to be independent of the material world, to resemble God and be eternal and purely spiritual; yet at the same time it recognises that it is a part of the material world, that its physical desires and its pains and pleasures are real and inescapable. As a result the unhappy consciousness is divided against itself. This conception should be familiar from the discussion of Hegel's attitude to Kant's ethics in the preceding chapter; on this occasion, it is Christianity rather than Kant that Hegel has in mind. Recall St Paul's 'The good which I want to do I fail to do; but what I do is the wrong which is against my will', and St Augustine's plea: 'Give me chastity and continence, but do not give it yet.'

Hegel's target is any religion which divides human nature against itself − and he asserts that this is the upshot of any religion which separates man from God, putting God in a 'beyond' outside the human world. This conception of God, he maintains, is really a projection of one aspect of human nature. What the unhappy consciousness does not realise is that the spiritual qualities of God which it worships are in fact qualities of *its own self*. It is in this sense that the unhappy consciousness is an alienated soul: it has projected its own essential nature into a place for ever out of its reach, and one which makes the real world in which it lives seem, by contrast, miserable and insignificant.

Reading Hegel's treatment of the unhappy consciousness in isolation from his other writings, one could well take him to be attacking all religion, or at the very least Judaism, Christianity and other religions based on a conception of God as a being distinct from the human world. He appears to be denying the existence of any such God, and explaining our belief in God as a projection of our own essential attributes. Only pantheism, or a humanism which takes humanity itself as divine, would be immune from this condemnation. Yet Hegel was, as we have seen, a member of the Lutheran Church, and in several of his other writings, including the *Philosophy of History*, and even in a later section of the *Phenomenology* itself, Protestant Christianity is viewed in a much more positive light. Did Hegel, in his later writings and his personal behaviour, compromise the radical thrust of his views about religion, as he appears to have compromised the radical thrust of his view of the State? After Hegel's death, a group of young radicals took this view of Hegel's philosophy. They saw themselves as following the true, uncompromised essence of his thought, and placed special emphasis on his discussion of the unhappy consciousness. We shall follow this sequel in the final chapter of this book.

Mind's goal

We shall now pass over a huge chunk of the *Phenomenology*. Some of what we are missing is tedious and obscure; other sections come close to equalling in interest and importance those we have just discussed. Sometimes the topics are just what one would expect to find in a philosophical work. There are discussions of the metaphysical ideas of Fichte and Kant. There is a critique of hedonism, or the pursuit of pleasure. There is a discussion of Kant's ethics, making objections similar to those we have already encountered in discussing the *Philosophy of Right*. Moral sentimentality of the type made popular in Hegel's time by the Romantic movement also comes in for critical analysis.

Other topics are more unusual. There is, for instance, a long section on physiognomy and phrenology – the pseudo-sciences based on the idea that one can tell people's character from (in the case of physiognomy) the shape of their faces or (according to phrenology) the bumps on their skulls. Hegel opposes these ideas, not because he has evidence of their inaccuracy, or any reason as mundane as that, but for the philosophical reason that mind is not to be tied to anything as material as a face or a skull.

Another unusual section is an analysis of a society built upon the *laissez-faire* economic theory of Adam Smith and his school, according to which each works to accumulate wealth for himself, but in fact contributes by his labours to the prosperity of the whole. Hegel's objection here — a point later to be taken up and made much of by both Marxist and non-Marxist critics of free-enterprise economics — is that by encouraging individuals to seek their own private interests, this economic system prevents individuals from seeing themselves as part of a larger community.

These diverse topics, along with many others, are woven into Hegel's conception of the path mind must travel in order to reach absolute knowledge. We have seen how he maintained that there could be no adequate knowledge without a self-conscious mind, and how self-consciousness was developed by working on the world and changing it. From that point on, Hegel sees all of human history as the development of mind. Historical periods such as Ancient Greece, the Roman Empire, the Enlightenment and the French Revolution have much the same significance as they do in the *Philosophy of History*. They are stages in the progress of mind towards freedom. So too are many of the elements of the organic community that Hegel described in the *Philosophy of Right*. Despite these broad similarities, there are some differences between the way Hegel treats this material in the *Phenomenology* and his later treatment in the *Philosophy of History* and the *Philosophy of Right*. I shall mention three.

The difference that strikes the reader at once is that in the *Phenomenology* no specific countries, periods, dates, events or people are named. While the references to specific periods and events are usually obvious enough — especially to the reader familiar with the *Philosophy of History* — everything is dealt with as if it were an instance of a general process that mind is forced to pass through by the inner necessity of its drive to self-realisation. It is as if references to specific people, times or places would somehow suggest that things might have turned out differently if the people or circumstances had been different.

Hegel manages to give the impression that the process he is describing would have occurred if the development of mind had taken place on Mars. Indeed, so abstract is the tone of the *Phenomenology*, so devoid of a sense of time and place, that if mind *had* developed on Mars, Hegel would not have had to change anything.

A second difference is that whereas both the *Philosophy of History* and the *Philosophy of Right* culminate in the achievement of a State resembling the Prussian form of monarchy, this type of State is not even mentioned in the *Phenomenology*. The sections that parallel the *Philosophy of History* end with the French Revolution. The French Revolution is a climax to history in the sense that it represents mind in a state of absolute freedom, aware of its ability to change the world and to mould political and social life according to its own will. For reasons similar to those offered in the *Philosophy of History*, Hegel portrays the abstract freedom of the French Revolution as leading inevitably to its opposite, the negation of the free self that is terror and death; but there is no further political development in the *Phenomenology*. Instead the path of mind moves to more rarefied levels, first to the moral view of the world advanced by Kant, Fichte and the Romantics, then to the religious state of mind, and finally to absolute knowledge itself, which is achieved by philosophy.

There is an obvious explanation for the absence of references to the Prussian State in the *Phenomenology*. When Hegel wrote it he was teaching not in Prussia, but at Jena. Moreover he wrote during the period of the Napoleonic wars, when France was the dominant power in Europe, and the future of the German States was unpredictable. So Hegel would have had to be remarkably prescient to anticipate the resurgence of the Prussian State and to make it the culmination of his political history. The understandable absence of references to some such State has naturally made the *Phenomenology* popular with those who believe that in his later works Hegel compromised his true views in order to please his political masters.

The third major difference between the *Phenomenology* and the later works is that in the *Philosophy of History* Hegel describes the course of history as nothing but the progress of the consciousness of the idea of freedom, whereas in the *Phenomenology* the emphasis is, as we have seen, on development towards absolute knowledge. Taking these terms in their ordinary senses, it would seem that in the two works Hegel takes different and incompatible views. Surely one can be knowledgeable while languishing in a tyrant's cell; and one can live in total freedom on a tropical island in blissful ignorance of all science, politics and philosophy. But by now we should know enough about Hegel to beware of taking his terms in their ordinary senses. For Hegel, absolute knowledge and true freedom are inseparable. Our final task, so far as the *Phenomenology* is concerned, is to understand what he means by absolute knowledge. To do this we first need to understand why the progress of the consciousness of the idea of freedom is also the progress of mind towards absolute knowledge.

Our earlier examination of Hegel's conception of freedom revealed that for him we are free when we are able to choose uncoerced by other people, by social circumstances, or by natural desires. That examination concluded with the promise that a better understanding of this view would emerge once we knew a little about his system of ideas as a whole. We have now learnt from the *Phenomenology* that Hegel sees all human history as the necessary path of the development of mind. The fact that he takes mind as the driving force of history indicates why he insists that our own desires, whether natural or socially conditioned, are a restriction on freedom. Freedom for Hegel is not freedom to do as we please: it consists in having a free mind. Mind must be in control of everything else, and must know that it is in control. This does not mean (as it did for Kant) that the non-intellectual side of nature is simply to be suppressed. Hegel gives our natural and socially conditioned desires their place, as he gives traditional political institutions their place; but it is always a place within a hierarchy ordered and controlled by mind.

The kind of freedom Hegel believes to be genuine is to be found, as we saw, in rational choice. Reason is the essential nature of the intellect. A free mind, unimpeded by coercion of any sort, will follow reason as easily as a river unimpeded by mountains or hills would flow directly to the sea. Anything that is an obstacle to reason is a limitation on the freedom of mind. Mind controls everything when everything is rationally ordered.

We also saw that Hegel regards reason as inherently universal. If reason is the essential medium of mind, it follows that mind is inherently universal. The particular minds of individual human beings are linked because they share a common universal reason. Hegel would put this even more strongly: the particular minds of individual human beings are aspects of something inherently universal, namely mind itself. The greatest obstacle to the rational ordering of the world is simply that individual human beings do not realise that their minds are part of this universal mind. Mind progresses towards freedom by chipping away at this obstacle. Remember how at the very beginning of the *Phenomenology* consciousness was limited to knowledge of the bare particular 'this', and was compelled to accept the universal terms implicit in language. From that point on, every step has been a step along a winding road that leads towards a mind closer to conceiving of itself as something both rational and universal. This is the road to freedom, because individual human minds cannot find freedom in rational choice when they are locked into conceptions of themselves that do not acknowledge the power of reason or its inherently universal nature.

Once this is understood, it is not difficult to see a connection between freedom and knowledge. All that needs to be said is that for human beings to be free, they must be fully aware of the rational and hence universal nature of their intellect. This self-awareness is absolute knowledge. As Hegel wrote in the *Philosophy of History*:

That the mind of the Egyptians presented itself to their consciousness in the form of a *problem* is evident from the celebrated inscription in the sanctuary of the Goddess Neith: '*I am that which is, that which was, and that which will be; no one has lifted my veil.*' . . . In the Egyptian Neith, truth is still a problem. The Greek God Apollo is its solution; his utterance is: '*Man, know thyself.*' In this dictum is not intended a self-recognition that regards the specialities of one's own weaknesses and defects: it is not the individual that is admonished to become acquainted with his idiosyncrasy, but humanity *in general* is summoned to self-knowledge.

Humanity in general, Hegel could well have added, is at the same time summoned to freedom.

Absolute knowledge

We have seen that the goal of the *Phenomenology* is absolute knowledge, and that this is linked with the goal of history being the consciousness of freedom. Self-knowledge is both a form of knowledge and the basis of Hegel's conception of freedom. Why, though, does Hegel describe self-knowledge as 'absolute knowledge'? Should we not say that self-knowledge is part of knowledge, but by no means the whole of it? Psychology, after all, is only one science among many; and even if we add to it anthropology, biology, history, evolutionary theory, sociology and all the other sciences that can contribute to our knowledge of ourselves, there will be many areas of knowledge entirely outside this category or at best very remotely linked to it: geology, physics, astronomy and so on. Are these not also part of absolute knowledge?

There are two misconceptions in this objection. One is easy to clear up. By 'absolute knowledge' Hegel does not mean knowledge of everything. Absolute knowledge is knowledge of the world as it really is, in contrast to knowledge of mere appearances. To gain absolute knowledge we do not have to know all the facts it is possible to know. It is the job of scientists to learn more and more about the universe. Hegel's aim was the philosophical goal of showing how real knowledge is possible, not the scientist's aim of increasing the knowledge we have.

The second misconception can only be eliminated by an explanation of Hegel's position on the nature of ultimate reality. Hegel described himself as an 'absolute idealist'. 'Idealism' in philosophy does not mean what it means in ordinary language: it has nothing to do with having lofty ideals or striving to be morally perfect. The philosophical term should really be 'idea-ism' rather than 'ideal-ism', for its sense is that it is *ideas*, or more broadly our minds, our thoughts, our consciousness, that constitute ultimate reality. The opposed view is materialism, which contends that ultimate reality is material, not mental. (Dualists believe that both mind and matter are real.)

Hegel believes, then, that the ultimate reality is mind, not matter. He also believes that the *Phenomenology* has led to this conclusion. From the stage of sense-certainty onwards, every attempt to gain knowledge of an objective reality independent of mind failed. The raw information received by the senses proved meaningless until it was brought under a conceptual system produced by consciousness. Consciousness had to shape the world intellectually, to classify and order it, before knowledge was possible. So-called 'material objects' turned out to be not things existing quite independently of consciousness, but constructs of consciousness, involving concepts like 'property' and 'substance'. At the level of self-consciousness, consciousness became aware of the laws of science as laws of its own creation, and so for the first time mind had itself as the object of its scrutiny. It was also at this stage that consciousness began to shape the world practically as well as intellectually, by taking material objects and working on them, fashioning them in accordance with its own images of how they should be. Self-consciousness then began to shape its social world too, a process culminating in the discovery that reason is sovereign over everything. In other words, although we set out merely to trace the path of mind as it comes to *know* reality, at the end of the road we find that we have been watching mind as it *constructs* reality.

Only on this conception of reality as the creation of mind can Hegel fulfil the undertaking he made in the introduction to the *Phenomenology*, to show that we can have genuine knowledge of reality. Remember how he poured scorn on all conceptions of knowledge as some kind of instrument for grasping reality, or as a medium through which we view reality. All these conceptions, he said, divide knowledge from reality. Kant, with his notion of the 'thing-in-itself' as for ever beyond knowledge, was obviously one of the targets of this criticism. In contrast, Hegel promised that the *Phenomenology* would reach a point 'where knowledge is no longer compelled to go beyond itself', where reality will no longer be an unknowable 'beyond', but instead mind will know reality directly and be at one with it. Now we can understand what all this meant: absolute knowledge is reached when mind realises that *what it seeks to know is itself*.

This point is the key to understanding the *Phenomenology* as a whole. It is probably the most profound of all the ideas of

Hegel that I am attempting to convey in this book, so let us go over it again.

Reality is constituted by mind. At first mind does not realise this. It sees reality as something independent of it, even as something hostile or alien to it. During this period mind is estranged or alienated from its own creation. It tries to obtain knowledge of reality, but this knowledge is not genuine knowledge because mind does not recognise reality for what it is, and so regards it as a mysterious thing beyond its grasp. Only when mind awakens to the fact that reality is its own creation can it give up this reaching after the 'beyond'. Then it understands that there is nothing beyond itself. Then it knows reality as directly and immediately as it knows itself. It is at one with it. As Hegel puts it in the concluding section of the *Phenomenology*, absolute knowledge is 'mind knowing itself in the shape of mind'.

Hegel has thus brought his gigantic work to a bold and brilliant conclusion. He has produced a startling solution to the fundamental problem of philosophy, and at the same time shown why history had to move along the paths it has in fact travelled. Whether his vast edifice stands solidly is another question; but even if it crumbles before our eyes, we cannot help admiring the breadth and originality of the design.

There is one feature of the design that your guide cannot resist pointing out. Ask yourself *when* absolute knowledge is achieved. The answer is, of course, that it is achieved as soon as mind understands that reality is its own creation and there is no 'beyond' for it to know. And when does this occur? Well, since this conception of reality is the upshot of Hegel's *Phenomenology*, it must occur when Hegel's own mind grasps the nature of the universe. On Hegel's view, mind comes to its final resting-place when he, Hegel, understands the nature of reality. There can scarcely be a more momentous conclusion to a work of philosophy. The closing pages of *The Phenomenology of Mind* are no mere *description* of the culmination of all human history: they *are* that culmination.

Two questions

So magnificent is Hegel's philosophical cheek that to question it seems petty. Nevertheless there are many questions that virtually ask themselves. I shall briefly consider two central ones.

The first concerns Hegel's idealism. We may admit that there can be no knowledge without an intellect that structures the raw information received by the senses. We may grant that human beings shape their world practically, as well as theoretically, by working on it. But even when all this and more is taken into account, there remains the stubborn conviction that there must still be *something* 'out there' independently of our experience of it. After all, to say that mind imposes its categories on the raw information it receives from the senses – on the 'this' that is immediately present to consciousness at the level of sense-certainty – is to presuppose that there is raw information coming from somewhere. Hegel can deny that this raw information amounts to knowledge, but he cannot deny that it suggests the existence of something outside mind itself. The same point holds even more obviously for the view that mind shapes the world practically by working upon it. Michelangelo may have thought of David, taken a lump of marble, and turned it into a statue that accorded with his thoughts; but he would not have got far if there had been no marble in the first place.

This line of thought (in the theoretical rather than the practical sphere) led Kant to postulate his unknowable 'thing-in-itself'. Hegel has made some acute criticisms of this idea, but has he really shown that we can do without it?

The second question also flows from Hegel's idealism. Some idealists are subjectivists. They maintain that what is ultimately real are one's *own* thoughts and sensations. Different minds may have different thoughts and sensations, and if they do, there is no possible way of judging the contents of one mind to be true and those of the other false – indeed on this view such classifications are meaningless, for they erroneously presuppose an objective reality beyond the thoughts and sensations of individual minds. Hegel rejects the view that there are countless different 'realities' corresponding to the countless different minds that exist. He calls his form of idealism *absolute idealism* to distinguish it from subjective idealism. For Hegel there is only one reality, because, ultimately, there is only one mind.

Now we have returned to the question with which our investigation of the *Phenomenology* began. If Hegel believes that there is only one mind, what on earth can he mean by 'mind'? He must mean some kind of collective or universal mind. In that case, would not 'spirit', with all its religious connotations, have been a better translation all along? Is not the idea of a collective mind fundamentally a religious idea? Should we not regard it as Hegel's conception of God?

Perhaps; but if we are in the end forced to this view, it will be with a better understanding of the ambiguities and uncertainties of Hegel's position than we would have had if we had opted for that translation from the start.

That there remain uncertainties about Hegel's conception of mind is undeniable. On the one hand, he needs the conception of a collective or universal mind not only to avoid a subjective form of idealism, but also to make good his vision of mind coming to see all of reality as its own creation. If there are millions of distinct individual minds, no single mind will be able to see much of reality as its own practical creation, for a large part of reality will consist of the practical creations of other minds. The manner in which mind conceives of the world before it has achieved absolute knowledge − as something independent of it and even hostile to it − will often prove to be no deception, but the literal truth. All this seems to force upon us an interpretation of Hegel that would understand his term 'mind' as some kind of cosmic consciousness; not, of course, a traditional conception of God as a being separate from the universe, but rather as something more akin to those Eastern philosophies which insist that All is One.

On the other hand Hegel regarded himself as a thoroughgoing defender of reason. Can we reconcile this with what he says, and needs to say, about mind? One way of doing so might be to take very seriously the extent to which Hegel believes consciousness to be necessarily social. From the first section of the *Phenomenology*, Hegel insists that knowledge is only knowledge if it can be communicated. The necessity of language rules out the idea of an entirely independent consciousness. As consciousness develops into self-consciousness, too, it must interact with other consciousnesses if it is to develop. In the end mind can only find freedom and self-understanding in a rationally organised community. So minds are not separate atoms, linked together by the accidents of association. Individual minds exist together, or they do not exist at all.

Hegel's social theory of mind is important, particularly for its influence on later thought, but it may not be enough to allow us to make sense of his idea of knowledge as mind at one with itself. There is still a second element to be drawn into service, however, and this is his idea of the universal nature of reason. We have already seen how Hegel regards reason as the essential principle of mind, and sees reason as essentially universal. He could therefore say: in so far as individual minds are truly mind — and not selfish or capricious desire — they really would all think and act in harmony with each other, they really would all recognise each other as having one and the same essential nature. This essential nature — this 'universal mind' — is neither an individual mind, nor a collective mind, but simply rational consciousness.

This may be an extreme and one-sided view of the nature of reason and of mind. It may be based, as I suggested his political philosophy might be based, on a misguided optimism about the possibility of harmony between human minds. It is not, however, a retreat into the mystical unity of a cosmic consciousness. Whether it is an accurate interpretation of the central message of the *Phenomenology* is another question.

5 Logic and dialectics

As I said in my preface, it is not my intention to give an exposition of Hegel's *Science of Logic*. On the other hand I do not wish to leave the reader with the mistaken impression that the *Logic* is an unimportant or peripheral work in the overall structure of Hegel's philosophy. I shall therefore say something about what Hegel set out to achieve in the *Logic*. In so doing I shall take the opportunity to explain that aspect of logic so frequently said to be Hegel's greatest discovery, the dialectical method.

Hegel's conception of logic

The goal of logic, Hegel tells us in the introduction to his *Science of Logic*, is truth. That is all very well, but what sort of truth? Hegel begins by referring to the traditional view of the subject, which begins with a separation between *form* and *content*, and takes logic to be the study of the form of true or valid thought, irrespective of its content. Logic as usually conceived studies forms of argument like:

> Everything that is A is B
>
> x is A
>
> Therefore x *is* B

Here we have a form without content. We could write 'human', 'mortal' and 'Socrates' for A, B and x respectively; or we could write 'four-legged animal', 'furry' and 'my pet tortoise'. The argument is valid in either case, though where there is a false premise, the conclusion may also be false. Validity is a matter of form, not content. To the logician the content is of no interest.

It follows from this separation of form and content that logic tells us nothing about the actual world. The forms of argument which logic describes would be exactly as they are if humans were immortal, or if tortoises were furry. They would not change if there were no humans or tortoises at all.

If we recall how in the *Phenomenology* Hegel began to investigate the problem of knowledge by challenging the commonly assumed distinction between the knower and what is known, it should come as no surprise to learn that Hegel mentions this traditional distinction between form and content only in order to deny it. Logic, he says, is the study of thought; but in his *Phenomenology of Mind* he has already shown that there is no objective reality independent of thought. Thought is objective reality, and objective reality is thought. Therefore when logic studies thought, it must also be studying reality. 'If we wish still to employ the word *matter*', he says, rubbing the point home, the content of logic is 'the true genuine matter'. He goes on to provide us with some images of the subject-matter of logic. It is, he says, 'the truth as it is, without husk in and for itself', or, to put it another way: 'this content shows forth God as he is in his eternal essence before the creation of nature and of a finite mind'.

Walter Kaufmann calls this 'perhaps the maddest image in all of Hegel's writings', but what it suggests is not entirely unrelated to the traditional view that logic tells us nothing about the world. In saying that logic is not about the world of nature and of finite minds, Hegel accepts part of the traditional view. The part he is most anxious to reject is the idea that reality, or truth, is to be found *only* in the world of nature and people. On the contrary, it follows from his absolute idealism that ultimate reality is to be found in what is mental or intellectual, not in what is material. It is to be found, to be specific, in rational thought. Logic is therefore the study of this ultimate reality in its pure form, abstracted from the particular forms it takes in the finite minds of human beings or in the natural world.

Hegel's view of mind as ultimate reality has a further consequence for the importance of logic. Since mind shapes the world, a study of rational thought will reveal the principles on which the world has been shaped. To put it in terms of Hegel's own image: to understand God's eternal essence before the creation of the world is to understand the basis on which the world was created.

The dialectical method

While working on a draft of *Capital* Marx wrote to Engels:

> In the *method* of treatment the fact that by mere accident I
> again glanced through Hegel's *Logic* has been of great service
> to me ... If there should ever be time for such work again, I
> would greatly like to make accessible to the ordinary human
> intelligence, in two or three printer's sheets, what is *rational*
> in the method which Hegel discovered but at the same time
> enveloped in mysticism ...

The method Marx is referring to is of course the dialectical
method, which Hegel describes as 'the only true method' of
scholarly and scientific exposition. It is the method he uses in
the *Logic* to uncover the form of pure thought.

Marx never found the time to write his explanation of what is
rational in the dialectical method. Many others did, however,
and they were by no means as brief as Marx had intended to be.
Some of these commentators build up dialectics into an alternative to all previous forms of logic, something that supersedes
such ordinary reasoning as the simple syllogistic form of
argument set out on the first page of this chapter. There is
nothing in Hegel to justify such extravagant claims for the
dialectical method. Nor is there any need to treat the dialectical
method, as others do, as something deep and mysterious. It is,
Hegel says, a method with a 'simple rhythm'; to dance to it
takes no great skill.

In our exposition of the *Phenomenology* we have in fact
already been doing the dialectical two-step, for that work is, as
Hegel tells us, 'an example of this method as applied to a more
concrete object, namely consciousness'. No one but Hegel could
think of consciousness as portrayed in the *Phenomenology* as a
relatively concrete object. But more concrete examples of the
dialectic are available in Hegel's later works, so for ease of
exposition let us begin with an instance from the *Philosophy of
History*.

In the *Philosophy of History*, one immense dialectical movement dominates world history from the Greek world to the
present. Greece was a society based on customary morality, a

harmonious society in which citizens identified themselves with the community and had no thought of acting in opposition to it. This customary community forms the starting-point of the dialectical movement, known in the jargon as the *thesis*.

The next stage is for this thesis to show itself to be inadequate or inconsistent. In the case of the community of ancient Greece, this inadequacy is revealed through the questioning of Socrates. The Greeks could not do without independent thought, but the independent thinker is the deadly foe of customary morality. The community based on custom thus collapses in the face of the principle of independent thought. It is now the turn of this principle to develop, which it does under Christianity. The Reformation brings acceptance of the supreme right of individual conscience. The harmony of the Greek community has been lost, but freedom is triumphant. This is the second stage of the dialectical movement. It is the opposite or negation of the first stage, and hence is known as the *antithesis*.

The second stage then also shows itself to be inadequate. Freedom, taken by itself, turns out to be too abstract and barren to serve as the basis for a society. Put into practice, the principle of absolute freedom turns into the Terror of the French Revolution. We can then see that both customary harmony and abstract freedom of the individual are one-sided. They must be brought together, unified in a manner that preserves them, and avoids their different forms of one-sidedness. This results in a third and more adequate stage, the *synthesis*. In the *Philosophy of History*, the synthesis in the overall dialectical movement is the German society of Hegel's time, which he saw as harmonious because it is an organic community, yet preserving individual freedom because it is rationally organised.

Every dialectical movement terminates with a synthesis, but not every synthesis brings the dialectical process to a stop in the way that Hegel thought the organic community of his own time brought the dialectical movement of history to an end. Often the synthesis, though adequately reconciling the previous thesis and antithesis, will turn out to be one-sided in some other respect. It will then serve as the thesis for a new dialectical movement, and so the process will continue. We saw this happen more than once in the *Phenomenology*. For example the section on consciousness concluded with the emergence of self-consciousness. Taking this as the thesis, we saw that self-consciousness needed some object from which to differentiate itself. The external object can be taken as the antithesis. This was unsatisfactory because the external object is something foreign or hostile to self-consciousness. The synthesis of these was desire, in which self-consciousness retains the external object, but makes it its own. The state of desire in turn proved (literally) unsatisfactory, and so we moved to an external object which was itself a self-consciousness. The second self-consciousness might be regarded as the antithesis of the first, and the synthesis of these two was a situation in which master was dominant over slave, thereby obtaining acknowledgement. This new synthesis proved no more lasting than its predecessors, for the slave ends up more independent and self-aware than the master. This antithesis found its synthesis in Stoicism, the philosophy of both master and slave . . . and so on.

In the *Logic* this same method is applied to the abstract categories in which we think. Hegel starts with the most indeterminate, contentless concept of all: being, or bare existence. Pure being, he says, is pure indeterminateness and vacuity. Pure being has in it no object for thought to grasp. It is entirely empty. In fact, it is nothing.

From this breathtaking beginning the dialectic of the *Logic* moves forward. The first thesis, *being*, has turned into its antithesis, *nothing*. Being and nothing are both opposites and the same; their truth, therefore, is this movement into and apart from each other — in other words, it is *becoming*.

So the dialectic leads on; but we shall not follow. We have seen enough to grasp the idea of the dialectical method. For Hegel it is a method of exposition, but it is a method that, Hegel says, 'is in no way different from its object and content — for it is the content in itself, *the dialectic which it has in itself*, that moves it on'. In the categories of our thought, in the development of consciousness, and in the progress of history, there are opposing elements which lead to the disintegration of what seemed stable, and the emergence of something new which reconciles the previously opposing elements but in turn develops its own internal tensions. This process is a necessary one,

because neither thought nor consciousness can spring into existence in an adequate form. They can achieve adequacy only by
the process of dialectical development. According to Hegel, the
dialectic works as a method of exposition because the world
works dialectically.

The absolute idea

Hegel's overriding aim in the *Logic* is straightforward: to
demonstrate the necessity of absolute idealism. He seeks to do
this by starting, as we have seen, from the bare concept of being,
and showing that this concept leads by dialectical necessity to
other concepts which more precisely and truly capture the
nature of reality; and these other concepts in turn prove inadequate and require others, until finally we reach 'the absolute
idea', of which Hegel says: 'Everything else is error and gloom,
opinion, striving, caprice and transitoriness; the absolute idea
alone is being, imperishable life, self-knowing truth, and the
whole of truth.' The *Logic* thus parallels the *Phenomenology*,
except that it moves in the realm of concepts instead of in the
realm of consciousness. Accordingly it has as its goal not
absolute knowledge, but the absolute idea itself. Whether it is
successful in proving the necessity of absolute idealism is something I shall not consider here, but one would have to search
hard to find a philosopher alive today who believes that Hegel
succeeds.

So what is 'the absolute idea'? That is not an easy question to
answer. Perhaps the best answer is: everything. That, however,
is not tremendously enlightening, so I shall try to be more
specific.

Hegel says that the absolute idea 'contains every determinate-
ness'. By that he means that it includes within itself every determinate or distinct thing — every human being, every tree, every
star, every mountain, every grain of sand. Nature and mind, he
says, are different ways in which its existence is manifested: they
are different forms of the absolute idea. Art and religion are
different ways of comprehending the absolute idea; or, to put it
exactly as Hegel does, art and religion are different ways in
which the absolute idea comprehends *itself*. (That it is self-
comprehension that is involved follows from the fact that

human beings are part of the absolute idea.) Philosophy, too, is a way of comprehending the absolute idea, but it is a higher form than art or religion because it grasps it conceptually, and consequently understands not only its own form of comprehension, but the aesthetic and religious forms as well.

It is of the essence of the absolute idea to manifest itself in distinct, limited forms, and then to return to itself. Self-comprehension is the form in which it returns to itself. This is the process we observed in the *Philosophy of History* and the *Phenomenology*, and now observe in the *Logic*. Self-comprehension becomes an objective social form in the ideal State described in the *Philosophy of Right*. In the *Lectures on Aesthetics* and the *Lectures on the Philosophy of Religion*, Hegel assesses the adequacy of various forms of art and religion as modes of comprehending the absolute idea. On the surface or lurking beneath, the self-comprehension of the absolute is the dominant theme of all Hegel's philosophy.

I have said that for Hegel the absolute is everything. I have also said that it seeks to comprehend itself. So we return again to the question we left unresolved at the conclusion of our discussion of the *Phenomenology*: does Hegel really believe that the universe as a whole, and everything in it, forms some kind of conscious entity? Is the absolute idea God?

It is clear that Hegel, notwithstanding his Lutheranism, was no orthodox Christian theist. The message of the section of the *Phenomenology* on 'the unhappy consciousness' is frequently repeated elsewhere in his works. To regard God as something apart from the world is to alienate the soul of man. If God exists, he is in the world, and human beings partake of his nature.

Then is Hegel a pantheist, one who asserts that God is simply identical with the world? This interpretation would be consistent with some of the things he says, but in the *Lectures on the Philosophy of Religion* Hegel explicitly rejects it, denying even that anyone has ever claimed that 'all is God'. Certainly Hegel does not think that particular things and finite human beings are literally God.

Could Hegel be an atheist, perhaps? We have seen that he places philosophy above religion as a means of comprehending the absolute idea. The Italian philosopher Benedetto Croce described Hegel's philosophy as 'radically irreligious, because it is not content to oppose itself to religion or to range it alongside of itself, but it resolves religion into itself and substitutes itself for it'. Croce was right to point to this sense in which Hegel's philosophy, in refusing to yield pride of place to religion, is deeply irreligious; yet there is so much else in Hegel's thought that is recognisably in the religious mould. There are his images and metaphors, like the one he used to describe the nature of the *Logic*. There is his philosophy of history, which is intended to illustrate how history works towards its goal under the direction of mind. There is also his view of ultimate reality as being able to comprehend itself, which suggests that ultimate reality is personal. To portray Hegel as an atheist is to go against some of his most central ideas.

Not an orthodox theist, not a pantheist, not an atheist — what else is left? Some years ago a Hegel scholar named Robert Whittemore argued that Hegel was a panentheist. The term comes from Greek words meaning 'all in God'; it describes the view that everything in the universe is part of God, but — and here it differs from pantheism — God is more than the universe, because he is the whole, and the whole is greater than the sum of all its parts. Just as a person is more than all the cells that make up his or her body — although the person is nothing separate from the body — so on this view God is more than all the parts of the universe, but not separate from it. Equally, just as no single cells amount to a person, so no individual parts of the universe amount to God.

Whittemore's interpretation is plausible, not only because it is consistent with what Hegel says specifically about God, but also because it makes sense of the dominant theme of his philosophy. If God is the absolute idea, the ultimate reality of the universe, the whole of its parts, we can understand why the absolute idea must manifest itself in the world, and there progress to self-comprehension. God needs the universe in the same way as a person needs a body.

The idea that God can lack anything is repugnant to most religious believers. That Hegel might be saying such a thing is, in their eyes, a reason for interpreting his philosophy as irreligious; but that is, I believe, a mistake. For Hegel sees God not as eternal and immutable, but as an essence that needs to manifest itself in the world, and, having made itself manifest, to perfect the world in order to perfect itself. It is a strange vision, but a powerful one. It is a vision that places immense weight on the necessity of progress: for the onward movement of history is the path God must take to achieve perfection. Therein may lie the secret of the immense influence that Hegel, for all his outward conservatism, has had on radical and revolutionary thinkers.

6 Aftermath

After Hegel's death, those who considered themselves his followers split into two camps. The orthodox or Right Hegelians followed in the style of Hegel's later years. They reconciled his religious views with Protestant Christianity, and accepted the generally positive view of the Prussian State expressed in the *Philosophy of Right*. This conservative school of Hegelianism produced no major thinkers, and after having for some years the status of a semi-official philosophy in Berlin, it went into so steep a decline that by the 1860s Hegel's philosophy was totally out of fashion in Germany.

The other camp was very different. It consisted of a group of young men with radical leanings. Their attitude to Hegel was like Hegel's attitude to Kant. Just as Hegel had seen Kant's doctrine of the thing-in-itself as a failure to carry through the radical implications of his philosophy, so these students of Hegel saw his acceptance of Christianity, the Prussian State, and the general conditions of their time as Hegel's failure to carry through the radical implications of *his* philosophy. This group became known as the Young Hegelians, or Left Hegelians. The future lay with them.

The Young Hegelians saw Hegel's philosophy as a demand for a better world, a world in which the opposition between individual and society would be overcome, a rationally organised world, a world of genuine freedom, in short a world fashioned to reflect the absolute supremacy of the human mind and its powers of reason. This better world was not, for the Young Hegelians, simply a Utopian ideal drawn up in a fanciful moment. It was the culmination of the historical and philosophical arguments of the Hegelian system. It was a dialectical necessity, a synthesis that would have to emerge to reconcile the conflicting elements of the world in which they lived.

Scorning the idea that Germany in the 1830s could be the fulfilment of the promise of Hegel's philosophy, the Young Hegelians set about finding ways of achieving their radical vision. At first they seized on religion as the crucial obstacle to a society that would allow human powers to reach their full potential. Developing the hints in the section of the *Phenomenology* on 'the unhappy consciousness', they argued that religion is a form of alienation. Man creates God, and then imagines that God has created him. Man puts into his image of God all that is best in himself: knowledge, goodness and power. Then man bows down before this image of his own making and sees himself, by comparison, as ignorant, sinful and weak. To restore human beings to their full powers, all that is needed is to make them realise that it is human beings who are truly the highest form of divinity.

To this end two Young Hegelians wrote books that had a tremendous impact on nineteenth-century thought about religion. David Friedrich Strauss wrote a brilliant *Life of Jesus* which, by treating the Gospels as source-materials open to historical criticism, set a model for all future study of the historical Jesus. Ludwig Feuerbach's *The Essence of Christianity* portrayed all traditional religion as man's projection of his own attributes into another sphere. It was thus the first modern attempt to develop a psychology of religious belief. Translated into English by Marian Evans (who also helped to translate Strauss, and is better known by her pseudonym George Eliot), the book had a world-wide impact at a time when Hegel's own writings were little known outside Germany.

The Young Hegelians then moved beyond religion. In a still more radical manner, Feuerbach turned Hegel's ideas against their author. He accused Hegel of having presented truths about the world in a mystified manner. Believing that mind is ultimately real, Hegel had seen the problem of disharmony in the world as a problem in the realm of thought, and so had believed that philosophy could solve it. Now Feuerbach inverted Hegel. Being is not to be derived from thought, but thought from being. Man does not have his true basis in mind: mind has its true basis in man. Hegel's philosophy is itself a form of alienation, for it takes the essence of real, living people to be something – 'mind itself' – outside themselves. We need neither theology nor philosophy, Feuerbach said, but a science which studies real people in their actual lives.

From here it is not far to the Young Hegelian through whose work elements of Hegel's thought were to have a lasting impact on the history of the world. Karl Marx came to the University of Berlin some six years after Hegel's death. He soon attached himself to the Young Hegelians and joined in the prevailing criticism of religion. When Feuerbach proclaimed the need to go beyond the realm of thought, Marx responded eagerly to the call. In his *Economic and Philosophical Manuscripts of 1844* Marx praised Hegel's *Phenomenology* for its account of alienation and of the importance of labour. He then developed his own view of labour under the capitalist system as the key form of alienation. To bring about the liberation of humanity, alienated labour must be abolished. To abolish alienated labour, Marx said, it is necessary to abolish private property and the wage system that goes with it: in other words, to institute communism.

In these youthful *Manuscripts* Marx describes communism in terms that all Hegelians would have found familiar:

> Communism . . . is the genuine resolution of the antagonism between man and nature and between man and man; it is the true resolution of the conflict between existence and essence, objectification and self-affirmation, freedom and necessity, individual and species. It is the riddle of history solved and knows itself as this solution.

As he grew older Marx used less Hegelian terminology, but he never abandoned the vision of communism he had reached through his transformation of Hegel's philosophy.

It is entertaining, if fruitless, to speculate on what thinkers long dead would say if they could return to life and see what has happened to their ideas. Few of them could be as startled as Hegel would have been to see that the historical culmination of his philosophy has not been comprehension of the absolute idea, but a vision of a communist society that for more than a hundred years has inspired revolutionary movements around the world.

Notes on sources

Each chapter of this book, apart from the first and the last, deals with one of Hegel's works. Here I shall provide references for passages I have quoted from these works, and from other sources. In every case the edition used is the one cited in the list of further reading which follows these notes. Where I have used several quotations from a single passage, only the first is identified; the others will then have been taken from the same or a closely following page. I have provided references for summaries and paraphrases only if the original passage is likely to prove difficult to locate.

Chapter 1: Hegel's times and life

Page 1. Hegel's comments on the French Revolution are from his *Philosophy of History*, p. 447.

Page 4. Hegel's estimate of Kant's importance comes from the *Science of Logic*, vol. I, p. 44.

Page 7. The description of Hegel lecturing is by H. G. Hotho and can be found in Walter Kaufmann, *Hegel*, pp. 350–1. Kaufmann's book also contains other documentation for the details of Hegel's life.

Chapter 2: History with a purpose

Page 9. Engels praised Hegel's sense of history in the course of a review of Marx's *Contribution to the Critique of Political Economy*, available in K. Marx and F. Engels, *Selected Works* (Foreign Languages Publishing House, Moscow, 1951), vol. I, pp. 337–8.

Page 11. The famous sentence setting out the goal of history occurs on p. 19 of the *Philosophy of History*. China and India are said to be 'outside' history on p. 116, and Persia is put at the beginning of true history on p. 173.

Page 15. Hegel's discussion of Socrates is on pp. 269–70.

Page 16. The distinction between the Persian and Roman Empires is set out on p. 278.

Page 17. For Hegel's account of the special nature of Christianity, see p. 333.

Page 19. 'a long, eventful and terrible night' is on p. 411.

Page 20. The essential principle of the Reformation is on pp. 416–17.

Page 21. The passage on the French Revolution is from p. 447.

Chapter 3: Freedom and community

Page 24. Schopenhauer attacked Hegel in the preface to the second edition of his major work, *The World as Will and Idea*. The passage is quoted by Popper in *The Open Society and Its Enemies*, vol. II, p. 33. Popper's own estimate of Hegel's aim is on the preceding page.

Page 25. Isaiah Berlin's 'Two Concepts of Liberty' is in his *Four Essays on Liberty* (Oxford University Press, London, 1969).

Page 26. Hegel's objection to the negative concept of freedom is in paragraph 15 of *The Philosophy of Right*.

Page 28. The comments on 'comfort' are from an 'addition' – that is, remarks added to the text by Hegel's editors, using notes taken by students at Hegel's lectures – to paragraph 191.

Page 32. The remark on duty is from paragraph 149; the one on Kant is from the addition to paragraph 133.

Page 34. Bradley's description is to be found in his *Ethical Studies* (first published 1876; republished by Oxford University Press, Oxford, 1962), pp. 171–2. The passage is quoted by Richard Norman, *Hegel's Phenomenology*, pp. 84–5, and I have used his condensation of it.

Pages 36–7. For the view of town planning used here to illustrate Hegel's idea of rationality, see Jane Jacobs, *The Death and Life of Great American Cities* (Random House, New York, 1961).

Page 38. Hegel sets out the constitutional arrangements of his rational State in paragraphs 291–2.

Page 40. For Hegel's views on freedom of expression, see paragraph 319; and on the jury system, 228. On the whole issue of the similarity between Hegel's State and the Prussian State of his time, see T. M. Knox, 'Hegel and Prussianism', in Walter Kaufmann (ed.), *Hegel's Political Philosophy*. This volume also contains a reply by E. F. Carritt.

Page 41. Popper marshals his quotations from Hegel on p. 31 of *The Open Society and Its Enemies*, vol. II. This method of presenting Hegel's ideas is attacked by Walter Kaufmann in 'The Hegel Myth and Its Method', available in *Hegel's Political Philosophy* and in Alasdair MacIntyre (ed.), *Hegel*. Kaufmann also points out the mistranslation of the sentence about the State. The German reads: 'es ist der Gang Gottes in der Welt, dass der Staat ist'. The sentence occurs in the addition to paragraph 258.

Page 42. 'the right of subjective freedom ...' is from paragraph 124, and 'What is of the utmost importance ...' from the addition to 265. In paragraph 215 Hegel insists that laws are not binding unless universally known.

Page 43. His attack on von Haller is the subject of a lengthy footnote to paragraph 258.

Chapter 4: The odyssey of mind

Page 48. Marx's reference to the *Phenomenology* is in his *Economic and Philosophical Manuscripts of 1844*, in D. McLellan (ed.), *Karl Marx: Selected Writings* (Oxford University Press, Oxford, 1977), p. 98.

Pages 48–9. The passages quoted here are from Hegel's introduction to *The Phenomenology of Mind*, pp. 131ff.

Page 51. The passage on Kant is from the section of the *Encyclopedia* on logic, published in English under the title *The Logic of Hegel*, paragraph 10. The passage is quoted by Norman, *Hegel's Phenomenology*, p. 11.

Page 54. For Hegel's view of proper names, see his *Science of Logic*, vol. I, pp. 104–5. The view is referred to by Ivan Soll, *An Introduction to Hegel's Metaphysics*, p. 97.

Page 55. The statement that what cannot be reached by language is untrue is from the *Phenomenology*, p. 160. For the various meanings of 'meinen', which I have translated as 'believed' in the sentence quoted, see Soll, *An Introduction to Hegel's Metaphysics*, p. 102.

Pages 61–2. For Marx's theory of alienated labour, see the section so titled in the *Economic and Philosophical Manuscripts of 1844*.

Page 62. 'In thinking I am free...' is on p. 243 of the *Phenomenology*.

Page 68. The passage quoted is from p. 220 of the *Philosophy of History*.

Page 71. 'Mind knowing itself...' is from the *Phenomenology*, p. 798.

Chapter 5: Logic and dialectics

Page 76. The metaphorical descriptions of the subject-matter of *The Science of Logic* are from that work, vol. I, p. 60. Kaufmann refers to Hegel's image on p. 195 of his *Hegel*.

Page 77. Marx's acknowledgement of the usefulness of the method of the *Logic* is quoted from a letter he wrote to Engels in 1858, reprinted in D. McLellan, *The Thought of Karl Marx* (Macmillan, London, 1971), p. 135. See also Marx's comments in the 'Afterword' to the second German edition of *Capital*: K. Marx, *Capital*, vol. I (Foreign Languages Publishing House, Moscow, 1961), pp. 19–20. A 'simple rhythm' is from the *Science of Logic*, vol. I, p. 65.

Page 81. Hegel's rejection of pantheism is to be found on p. 97 of the first volume of the *Lecture on the Philosophy of Religion*.

Page 82. Benedetto Croce's description of Hegel as 'radically irreligious' is from *What is Living and What is Dead in the Philosophy of Hegel?*, pp. 70–1. Robert Whittemore's 'Hegel as Pantheist' appeared in *Tulane Studies in Philosophy*, vol. IX (1960), pp. 134–64.

Further reading

Hegel's works

The standard German edition of Hegel's collected works is the twenty-volume Jubilee Edition, edited by H. Glockner and published in Stuttgart from 1927–30. For the English-speaking reader wondering where to begin reading Hegel's own works, I would recommend following the order of the works discussed in this book. English translations of these works are:

Lectures on the Philosophy of History, tr. J. Sibree (Dover, New York, 1956). The Introduction to these lectures is available separately, as *Reason in History: A General Introduction to the Philosophy of History*, tr. R. S. Hartman (Library of Liberal Arts, New York, 1953), and as *Lectures on the Philosophy of World History, Introduction: Reason in History*, tr. H. B. Nisbet (Cambridge University Press, Cambridge, 1975). The latter edition contains additional scholarly material.

Hegel's Philosophy of Right, tr. T. M. Knox (Oxford University Press, London, 1967).

The Phenomenology of Mind, tr. J. B. Baillie (Harper & Row, New York, 1967). There is also a more recent and, in the view of many, more reliable translation by A. V. Miller, entitled *Hegel's Phenomenology of Spirit* (Oxford University Press, Oxford, 1977).

Hegel's Science of Logic, tr. W. H. Johnston and L. G. Struthers in two volumes (Allen & Unwin, London, 1929); also more recently translated by A. V. Miller (Allen & Unwin, London, 1969).

Probably the most important of Hegel's other works is his *Encyclopedia of the Philosophical Sciences*. This work has been published in English in its separate components. The section on logic, sometimes called the 'Lesser Logic', was translated by W. Wallace and published under the confusing title *The Logic of Hegel* (Clarendon Press, Oxford, 1874). There is now a new edition, with a foreword by J. N. Findlay (Clarendon Press, Oxford, 1975). The second part is available as *Hegel's Philosophy of Nature*, tr. A. V. Miller (Clarendon Press, Oxford, 1970) and also in a translation by M. J. Petry (Allen & Unwin, London, 1970). Wallace's original translation of *Hegel's Philosophy of Mind* (Clarendon Press, Oxford, 1894) has been republished, together with additional material translated by A. V. Miller (Clarendon Press, Oxford, 1971).

English translations of Hegel's other writings are:

Early Theological Writings, tr. T. M. Knox (University of Chicago Press, Chicago, 1948). This volume contains the earliest of Hegel's surviving works.

Hegel's Political Writings, tr. T. M. Knox (Clarendon Press, Oxford, 1964). Hegel's occasional political essays, such as that on the English Reform Bill, are collected here.

Lectures on the Philosophy of Religion, tr. E. B. Speirs and J. B. Sanderson, in three volumes (Routledge & Kegan Paul, London, 1968).

Hegel's Aesthetics, tr. T. M. Knox, in two volumes (Clarendon Press, Oxford, 1975).

Lectures on the History of Philosophy, tr. E. S. Haldane and F. H. Simson, in three volumes (Routledge & Kegan Paul, London, 1955).

Books about Hegel

For readers wishing for further guidance I would recommend Richard Norman's slim and stimulating volume, *Hegel's Phenomenology: A Philosophical Introduction* (Sussex University Press, Brighton, 1976). Next could come Ivan Soll, *An Introduction to Hegel's Metaphysics* (University of Chicago Press, Chicago, 1969). After that one might move on to the shorter of Charles Taylor's two books on Hegel, *Hegel and Modern Society* (Cambridge University Press, Cambridge, 1979), or, if one is ready for it, to the much longer and more difficult *Hegel* (Cambridge University Press, Cambridge, 1975). For a detailed recent study of Hegel's *Phenomenology*, see Robert Solomon, *In the Spirit of Hegel: A Study of Hegel's Phenomenology* (Oxford University Press, New York, 1983).

Older, but still useful works are: Edward Caird, *Hegel* (Blackwood, Edinburgh, 1901); Benedetto Croce, *What is Living and What is Dead in the Philosophy of Hegel?*, tr. D. Ainslie (Russell & Russell, New York, 1969); W. T. Stace, *The Philosophy of Hegel* (Dover, New York, 1955); and J. N. Findlay, *Hegel: A Re-examination* (Allen & Unwin, London, 1958).

Information on Hegel's life, together with translations of many letters and other documents, can be found in Walter Kaufmann, *Hegel* (Weidenfeld & Nicolson, London, 1965). *Hegel's Development* by H. S. Harris (Clarendon Press, Oxford, 1972) is the best study of Hegel's early years. The influential work by George Lukacs, *The Young Hegel*, is now available in an English translation by R. Livingstone (Merlin Press, London, 1975).

Several interesting books have been written specifically on Hegel's social and political ideas. These include: Herbert Marcuse, *Reason and Revolution* (Humanities Press, New York, 1954); Shlomo Avineri, *Hegel's Theory of the Modern State* (Cambridge University Press, Cambridge, 1972); Raymond Plant, *Hegel* (Allen & Unwin, London, 1973); and Judith Shklar, *Freedom and Independence: a Study of the Political Ideas of Hegel's 'Phenomenology of Mind'* (Cambridge University Press, Cambridge, 1976). Some heated exchanges over the extent to which Hegel's philosophy supports the authoritarian State have been collected by Walter Kaufmann in a volume entitled *Hegel's Political Philosophy* (Atherton Press, New York, 1970). There is also a collection of articles edited by Z. Pelczynski, entitled *Hegel's Political Philosophy* (Cambridge University Press, Cambridge, 1971). Together with this one might read – though with considerable caution – Karl Popper's provocative attempt to find the origins of totalitarianism in Hegel's thought: see *The Open Society and Its Enemies*, vol. II, chapter 12 (Routledge & Kegan Paul, London, 1966).

For further study of the religious aspect of Hegel's thought, see Emil Fackenheim, *The Religious Dimension of Hegel's Thought* (Indiana University Press, Bloomington, 1967), and Bernard Reardon, *Hegel's Philosophy of Religion* (Macmillan, London, 1977). See also Robert C. Whittemore's article, 'Hegel as Panentheist' in *Tulane Studies in Philosophy*, vol. IX (1960), pp. 134–64. This volume is a special issue on Hegel.

There are innumerable scholarly articles on Hegel in the philosophical journals. Some of the best have been collected in Alasdair MacIntyre (ed.), *Hegel: A Collection of Critical Essays* (Anchor, New York, 1972).

Finally, the various transformations of Hegel's thought by the Young Hegelians are well described in Sidney Hook, *From Hegel to Marx* (Humanities Press, New York, 1958), and also in David McLellan, *The Young Hegelians and Karl Marx* (Macmillan, London, 1969).

Index